Aristah Noble is the pseudonym for a writer you've never heard of before. She has been writing her entire life, but never had the courage to share her experiences with the world, until now.

Aristah spends her time reading, writing, stargazing, and baking, all while deftly avoiding politics and scorpions.

This book is dedicated to my bears. Mama bear, sister bear, brother bear. We've been through it, haven't we? I love you from the bottom of my whole soul.

Aristah Noble

CHOCK FULL OF FUCKERY

AUSTIN MACAULEY PUBLISHERS™

LONDON • CAMBRIDGE • NEW YORK • SHARJAH

Ordering Information
Quantity sales: Special discounts are available on quantity purchases by corporations, associations, and others. For details, contact the publisher at the address below.

Publisher's Cataloging-in-Publication data
Noble, Aristah
Chock Full of Fuckery

ISBN 9798889107880 (Paperback)
ISBN 9798889107897 (ePub e-book)

Library of Congress Control Number: 2023924122

www.austinmacauley.com/us

First Published 2024
Austin Macauley Publishers LLC
40 Wall Street, 33rd Floor, Suite 3302
New York, NY 10005
USA

mail-usa@austinmacauley.com
+1 (646) 5125767

This book is the product of being hated and harmed, of being loved and healed. Of not believing I was enough. Of finally understanding that I was all I needed to be.

Thank you to my family and friends. For loving me, healing me, and for caring about me when I couldn't do it for myself. For every step you've taken with me. You make it all worthwhile.

Thank you to the assholes who tried to break me. You lost. You don't matter. I thrived in spite of you. Enjoy your abysmal existence. GFYD.

Thank you to the entire Austin Macauley Publishers team for taking a chance on me. It's still a bit of a shock.

Table of Contents

A Stranger's Hand	15
Epiphany	16
Hello	17
Power	19
Distance	20
My Choice	21
Forged	23
Castle Party	24
Trade	26
Why You Cuss So Much?	29
On Earth	30
Without Her	32
Oh Toronto	34
Suspicious	36
Perspective	38
Poison	39
Daybreak	40
Memory Tree	41
The Trees of My Childhood	43
Star Wars	44
Waiting	45
Speaking of Dating... Nice Segue, Huh?	47
Wilted	49
Sleep	51
Consume	52
War	55
Cliché	58
Grave Clothes	60

What's Your Fantasy? 62

Still 63

Can't Fly 64

The Wire 65

Partial-ly 66

Steri-Strips 67

Don't 70

Dragon 72

Beige 75

Dangerous Angel 81

Dating Is a Bitch 83

Charcoal 85

Swing 87

I Love You 88

Absolution 89

Killer 91

At Rest 93

Screenshots 95

Zero 97

Thanks-Giving! 98

Holi-Daze 100

Reese's 102

Dead to Me 103

Come In 104

A Friend Request 106

My Friend, My Brother 108

In Love 110

Threnody 111

Gram-er? 113

Surcease 114

Burn 115

Winter	116
Unmade	117
Get Off	118
Go	119
Chair	120
Steps	121
For You	123
Swallowed	124
Torch	125
Smile	126
Ice Queen	127
What's Up	128
Game Over	130
Goat	131
UberXL	132
Captive Audience	134
The End	135

Hello!

This is a small peek at my life, at a woman many choose to misinterpret and misunderstand. This is me. Talking to you. In chaotic fashion. There are no clever turns of phrase, no style, no great revelations. Poems, micro-sized short stories, burning questions, and other stuff because squirrel brain. That's who I am.

It's chock full of fuckery. Like one of those weird-ass, late-night rambling conversations you have about nothing and everything.

Don't worry. I did **not** quit my day job. I'm not looking for sympathy. I know my ability, or lack thereof here. I just felt like this needed to happen. Catharsis.

I tend to string too many adjectives together, I overuse so & and, plus I say dude and fuck too much. As you see, I cuss. If that's a problem for you, stop reading.

People will hate this. They'll take to social media and keyboard cowboy, or girl, themselves to death. They'll make Tiktoks, if it isn't banned by now, and YouTube videos! They'll be full of derision, disdain, and lengthy treatises on why this is the worst thing they've ever read. They'll be so smug and gleeful. Have a go, keyboard cowpeople. Have. A. Go. I'm already laughing at you.

Burning question: Why *are* there such miserable fucks in this world? Guess what? If you don't like something, you don't have to go to great lengths to tell everyone in the most blistering terms possible. You can absolutely keep it to your gotdamn self. But you get off on that false feeling of power, don't you? Yeah, you do. Go step on a Lego.

Anyway. This isn't for any miserable fucks. It's for me. And you, too, if you want it to be. It's anyway, *not* anyways.

Write to me: *dacurlylife@gmail.com.* Hop on my new Facebook page, Aristah Noble.

No responses will be given to creeps, trolls, or assholes which leads me to my life's motto:

"When we meet, be you friend, family, lover, or pope, I shall give you a rope. Use it as you choose. Lifeline or noose." That's an original!

I'm not into necrophilia so once you're dead, you DED.

And hey
Guess what?
You're not fat
You're not stupid
You're not ugly
You're not too tall
You're not too short
You're not too skinny
Your hair isn't too curly (or straight)
Your boobs aren't too small
Your ass isn't too big
Your dick doesn't hang funny
You're not a slut
You're exactly as you should be

*I share this because I used to be a 00 at 5'9. I looked like a dollar store coat hanger. You wouldn't believe how many people called me fat when I got up to a whopping size 6! "Oh my God, you've gained so much weight! You're so big!" They had nothing to say to me except how "big" I'd gotten. At first, it bothered me. For the wrong reasons. I actually worried that I was fat. Ugh! At size six? Well, I woke up one day and chose violence. I would respond based on whether or not I wanted to burn the bridge. FYI? I burned **a lot** of bridges. These were some of the same motherfuckers who said, "Oh my God, you're way too skinny! Do you even eat?"*

"That musty moose knuckle suggests you might be gaining a lil weight too."
"I am very healthy, very happy, and I love my body."
"Your boyfriend loves my weight. Especially on his face."
Don't entertain people who try to slyly chip away at you. Serve them a hot cup of shut the fuck up.

If you're healthy, anyone telling you shit like this is lacking something in themselves. They're jealous. Bitter. Trying to steal your peace, your confidence in yourself. Tell them to fuck right off. And keep fucking off. Don't let anyone tear you down. NOT EVER. No one has that right. There are no perfect people in this universe. Nope. Not a one, ba-by! And for the sake of sanity don't dim your own shine. NEVER. Speak to yourself with positivity, kindness, and respect. Don't fuck it up like I used to.

You're perfect. You're enough.

Wear the tank top, the two-piece, the mini-skirt. Have tattoos or don't. Wear make-up or don't. Be he, she, they. Be gay. Be straight. Be Christian. Be Buddhist. Be an Atheist. Like whatever music, food, clothes, people, you want. You're the only one you have to answer to. Listen to 2Pac. Keep ya head up. Stroll your sexy ass all over this universe with a big smile on your face.

You're too amazing, kind, wonderful, funny, glorious, and fantastic to give energy to bitter, jaded, hateful ass carbon forms.

A Stranger's Hand

Written on this page
Are words
That make no sense
Black on white
Written plainly
Yet there's a nothingness
No beginning no end
No pattern or design
Can I define
No logic rises to defend
I wonder what this is
Some abstract reflection?
The state of a mind, twisted?
Some misguided attempt
At revelation
What do these words say?
What thought do they convey?
Was the writer happy, sad
Mad or pleased?
Faced with this mystery
I'm ill at ease
No clues light my path
And yet
The obsession to identify
Intensifies with each breath
Becomes a hunger
I don't understand
If I smash my head on this desk
Will it bring me clarity?
Or at least, a release?
From this wretched, evil, torturous sheet
This impenetrable, inscrutable, piece of unknown
That, so strangely
Was not penned
By a stranger's hand
But my own

Sometimes I look back at something I've written and have zero recollection of writing it. I wonder what the F could have been going on in my head, what happened that day, what I ate. Nothing comes up. It makes me feel a little crazy.

I don't drink heavily, don't smoke, don't do any drugs. Can't chalk it up to an altered state. This is just my brain on itself. Don't be like that. It's not that weird. There's no raven with his beak at my door. Who knows where the fuck my brain goes.

Epiphany

Bring me an epiphany
In a brightly colored bag
Decorated with bows
And a shiny new tag
So that I too
May know
The joy of discovery

If I could discover where this came from, that would be magic! Can you even get a bag with an epiphany in it? If you find one, please send it my way. Scratch that, send me cookies and Star Wars stuff. No Jar-Jar and no Ewoks, though. I have standards.

Hello

Hello my love
I need to tell you so much
But first, please, let me say
I'm sorry
For the shit I put you through
For the awful people I exposed you to
For not putting you first
For letting you be abused
For not giving you my all
For doubting you
For not trusting, not listening
For not trying to understand
For not giving you any space
For pushing you to ridiculous lengths
For ignoring your pain
For blocking your growth
For fucking you over
I'm sorry for all the worry,
The stress, and tears
I'm sorry for the lies
Sorry that I didn't hold you
Way up high
I'm sorry I constantly let you down
But I promise
Right now, and forever
To give you the best
Of my heart, soul, spirit, and mind
To open my ears and eyes
To love you like you deserve
I will put in the work
I will make mistakes
But never again
Will anything or anyone
Usurp the place
Reserved only for you
I love you with all that I am
And I will damn sure prove it

Surprise, surprise. I made this pledge to ME. I realized how responsible I was for much of my own sorrow, anger, and misery. I ignored who and what I am. I didn't trust myself. I listened to people who were invested in seeing me suffer. People who thrived from my pain. People so rotten and miserable they didn't know any other way to be.

Sometimes it hurts, these brick upside your head realizations, and it's easy to deny your own culpability. It's easy, but it's wrong. I don't always get it right, but I try. I try, I fail, I do it all over again. Every single day.

Power

Your brilliance
Leaves me blind
But I don't mind it
I soak in your glory
While you patently ignore me
Bowed, cowed, and awed
I stare longingly
Toward your face
Yet you refuse
Even my name
Still, you are the reason
I am awake
Your brazen forays
Into my soul
Allow me no break!
I greet you daily
With a private smile
And light in my eyes
That you never see
But I don't care
If you don't realize
I'm there
Your power over me
Wielded so casually
Is nonetheless complete

I don't remember when I wrote this or why. I found it on a thumb drive I had. I imagine I caught a stunning sunrise somewhere, but don't hold me to that. I could easily be talking out my ass about something else entirely. Sorry, but it's going to be like this the whole way through.

Distance

A long flight
An impossible drive
The salty sea
Separate you from me
But it doesn't matter
Distance has no meaning
The sun and moon
Know my feelings
I still feel your heart
Beating in time with mine
I still hold you
In my arms each night
Even though it's just a dream

Allergies were killing me at home. KILLING. I love outside but couldn't go out. Daily low-grade headache, runny nose, itchy eyes, sneezing, hives, sore throat, etc.

Something happens to us when we feel sick all the time. I found myself being edgy and irritable and honestly just a crusty bitch. Hiding it did not work.

After trying every drug, every home remedy, and being fucking exhausted, I moved to Arizona. I didn't talk to anyone about it because I knew I wouldn't do it and I would slowly go insane(r). The allergies are all better, but there's a place in my heart that will forever ache a little. I love my home and the people there. I miss them every day.

Yeah, there's no sea between but it rhymed. Sue me.

My Choice

"You're too black!"
"You're too white!"
"You need to choose!"
"Pick a side!"
Oh, I do?
Well fuck that
And fuck you too
Ice Cube style
Why should I
Identify to satisfy
Your diseased, narrow
Revolting little mind?
Bitch please
My fantastic construction
Won't be denied
Destruction
Obtained through fear
Ain't happening here
You can't cut me in two
And choose which half
You want to say hi to
And when you find
Another party in the bloodline
Will you split me in three?
Go away!
Your dissonance and nonsense
Is vile and repugnant
Stop trying to dissect
Simply accept or don't
I couldn't care less
My decision, my choice
Is to be exactly who I am
Without your labels or tags
Shove that box up your ass
I don't need you
Or your approval
I am **everything**
I want to be
I exist solely for *me*
Beginning to end
So yeah, fuck you again

I have been called every racist name. Albino, nigger, honkey, oreo, skunk, mud, coon, gator bait, shandy. The list is much bigger than this and I don't need to see it all in print.

I've been told I'm an abomination, a sin against God, that I should have never been born. That I'm pretty for a black girl. That I sound white. That I needed to pick a side. That I might end up being pretty enough that I wouldn't have to date 'the blacks'. That I shouldn't date outside my race.

I've been spit on, slapped, punched, kicked. Outside of my home, and with rare exception, I was abused or excluded.

I've never been in the clique, never been the IT girl. Always and forever on the outside. It used to make me terribly sad.

I could have turned into some hunched, crumpled, broken, hateful, bitch. I didn't. I won't say I always handled it well. That would be a lie. I had periods of crippling sadness and alternating rage. I may or may not have hit back a time or two. I may have made some horrible choices, done some hurtful things. No bueno.

Now? All the cool kids are doing it. Suddenly, and seemingly out of nowhere, I'm attractive and oh so interesting! So exotic! Best of both worlds! Uh-huh.

Truth is, I'm beyond glad for it. I never want another little girl or boy to feel the sadness, fear, anger, isolation, rejection, humiliation, pain, worthlessness...get your thesaurus for all the horrible feelings I experienced. Never.

Forged

By hammered fists
Daggered words
And heat of scorn
I was forged
A broken, cowering thing
Was desired
Yet denied
Because you got me
Flesh and steel
Strength and purpose
I was forged
And I will break *you*

Strides have been made, my loves. Please don't stop. The stories that go with this hurt. They hurt deep and they hurt hard. How many times can I say Vol II before you want to choke me? But that outside thing? I kinda like the view better out here.

Oh. Ice Cube style means with zero lube and a lot of fire.

Castle Party

Threw a castle party today
Akon showed up; I was Blown Away
Jimmy, John, John, and Robert
Came and took the pain
But like a Fool in the Rain
I let the Phantom and Webber
Go Down Once More
Into the cellar
To get me some wine
It opened up my mind
Enough for Lupe
To show me the Sunshine
Amy invited Valerie but
She couldn't cross the water
I told Ty and the guys to Come on By
And Glenn brought along his Mother!
Eric advised me I had him on his knees
But I'm not Layla!
My confusion was intense
So I spent some extra time
With that Sexy MF Prince
Mmm, mmm, mmmm
Got myself a Kiss
Tchaikovsky was giving lessons
In 1812 history
While Eddie skillfully played
Croquet in the Garden
Croce approached me with
Photographs and Memories
And Stevie was throwing
Ribbons in the Sky
So Jimi, Mr. Dylan, and I
Stood All Along the Watchtower
To watch them fly, when suddenly
O'Shea saw a Predator in the basin!
So Nina bade us all come in
"Wild Is The Wind, children!"
Though it took Ray to state
Baby It's Cold Outside
Before I moved my behind
We went inside and ate
Jack's Banana Pancakes
Which were great, yet
The hour was growing late

Giddy and heavy lidded
I heard as Sarah said
While you aren't *my* Little Man
You've Had a Busy Day
It's time for bed
I knew she was right
Thus I bid my guests goodnight
Anthony and Flea lectured me
About the Power of Equality
Until their chariot came
And slowly
My lovely guests rode away
Chuckling, I put myself to sleep
Hearing their voices in my head

If I have one addiction, it's music. I listen to almost everything. I was sitting in a chair with my iTunes on random. Pavarotti and Prince, System of a Down and Sinatra, Garth Brooks and Guns N Roses, Tupac and Tesla. You never know what will come up. Nothing else to it. Barely makes any sense. I couldn't care less.

That's your subtle reminder that the phrase is "I couldn't care less." If you could care less, then you would. Make sense?

And of course, I had to have a castle. Of course!

There's a list of the songs/artists in the back.

Trade

The lake is calm
Barely a ripple
Mars its surface
The breeze is light
The sun is warm
The birds, quiet
This place is serene
Beautiful, perfect, clean
But the filthy storm
Seething deep inside me
Refuses to be soothed
Rebukes the harmony
Spurns the tranquility
It speaks to me
 Harsh and discordant
Blot out the sun!
Disturb the lake!
Crush the birds!
Feed me!
I am very much drawn
To these hostile stirrings
The bleak negativity seduces
Still, I am only a woman
Angry, and hateful, yes
But I will never
Know true rage
This tranquil breeze
Could turn, and
Strip the skin from my back
While the sun scorched it black
These birds? HA!
They would use my hair
To line their nests
While my dead eyes
Stared wide
And this lake,
This calm quiet lake
Would swallow my soul
And carry me away
Never to be seen
I think it best
If I request a trade
Dearest lake

May I please
Sit at your feet
While the sun and breeze
Wash through me
Let me hear the birds sing
Let me leave my rage
To your embrace
Let *me* be beautiful, perfect, clean
Let me be free
Of these vicious feelings
And in return
I promise to cleave
To the version of me
Who recognizes the strength
The gift and magnificence
Of your peaceful beneficence

Remember that rage I talked about? Being in a rage about the things I went through never helped. It merely made my problems worse. I was so bent on lashing out to heal my pain. To inflict hurt. Instead of, I don't know, actually finding real ways to heal my pain.

I could be a real asshole. I was dealing from a place of sadness, anger, ignorance, and youth. I did hateful things. I probably missed out on a few deserved ass whoopins in my time too.

It was only in moments when I could calm down that I found answers or peace. Being around powerful things—lakes, oceans, mountains—were a salve to my spirit. I realized I could rage until my death, but I would never be as powerful or impactful as they were at their calmest.

BUT! It's not always easy. Some people won't let you be kind and calm. Fuck those people, though. With a hot screwdriver.

Do you feel like you're on a backward roller coaster designed by some drug addled, contrary, curly-headed psycho? It's okay if you like it.

Sidebar! I wonder if it's worse when people lie about me or when they tell the truth.

Lie! I don't wonder. There's so much vulnerability in the truth. People use lies to hurt, but the truth is infinitely more powerful. The truth of me is something I hold close and don't share with everyone. Very few people in this world truly know me.

When I was younger, people decided I was always either lying or flat out wrong. The sky was never blue, grass was not green. It got to the point where I would start saying blatant and obviously false things. I wanted to give them a real reason to hate me. To not believe me. I wanted them to stay away. Of course, I realized the folly in that! But I didn't care! I was a teenage girl with a swirling mixture of hurtful, confusing, destructive emotions inside. Toxic city. It caused unimaginable hurt to me in the end. Vol II.

These days, IDGAFF what anyone thinks or says about anything I do, think, feel, eat, wear. Ahh, the joy of being a whole, grown ass, secure woman.

Oh. That other f is flying.

Why You Cuss So Much?

I know cussing offends people. They always want to know why I cuss so much/have to cuss at all. It's simply because I do. Listen, I'm not chillin' at home wondering how many fucks I can insert into my conversations. I don't cuss around people I care about who I know are offended by it.

I was alone a lot, so I read the dictionary growing up. Still do. I know a whole *bunch* of fancy words. I just use the words that make the most sense to me. Fuck makes a lot of sense a lot of the time. Plus, the life I've lived gives me an allowance of never expiring fucks to sprinkle where I wish.

On Earth

January 23, 2025: Earth's scientists caught a glimpse of a large, fast-moving object via the James Webb Space Telescope. The object was nearing Saturn's moon, Titan, and appeared to be on a collision course with the planet.

The scientific community gnawed, worried, studied, postulated, and secretly rejoiced. NASA prepared. Feeds from the telescope were monitored around the clock.

Observatories around the world focused. The citizens of Earth bought toilet paper. All of it.

January 24, 2025–August 15, 2025: Revelations, Ragnarök, the Hour, Thanos. End of times. Hoax.

Government conspiracy. Skeptics and fanatics alike scanned the sky. For months, the inhabitants of Earth watched and waited as the object moved through the cosmos.

August 16, 2025: The object vanished. The skeptics were celebratory and smug. The fanatics continued to wail.

Scientists were deflated.

August 19, 2025: The object startled researchers at Mauna Kea Observatory by suddenly appearing just beyond the Earth's moon. It was clearly a spacecraft of some sort. It was huge. Mass panic ensued.

August 24, 2025: Eight million humans had been shot, stabbed, bludgeoned, trampled, burned, crushed, drowned, poisoned, and defenestrated. By other humans. The injured count was astronomic. The spacecraft loomed.

August 25, 2025: Martial law was put into effect all over the world. The military mobilized.

August 28, 2025: The entire planet was locked down. People are hunkered in their homes from Cincinnati to Perth. Suicide numbers rose.

August 31, 2025: The spacecraft entered the Earth's atmosphere at approximately 1:34 AM. It descended quickly and hovered over the Pacific, near the Mariana Trench. The world's entire military rushed out to meet it. Attempts to communicate with the craft were unsuccessful.

September 28, 2025: The craft continued to hover. The entire world was in chaos.

October 31, 2025: There was never a response from the spacecraft. It disappeared at 10:43 AM.

Population of Earth January 24, 2025: 11.2 billion

Population of Earth November 1, 2025: 7 billion

Aboard the Spacecraft

January 23, 2025: Dude! Slow down. Mom is going to kill us for taking the ship out. Do you even know where we are? We're gonna get grounded. We gotta get home before she gets off work. Oh my Zeve! You're gonna hit Saturn. No! I don't think you should push that!

August 19, 2025: Oh crap. We jumped. We are never getting off punishment. Never. I should have never listened to you. You are so stupid! *What planet is that?* Oh crap.

Oh crap. Is the shield up, or can they see the ship?

August 31, 2025: Whoa! I think those are humans down there. That's gotta be Earth! Can you believe it? Humans! I wonder how we can talk to them? We can't open the door from up here. Should we land? What do you mean you don't know how? You are so stupid! I'm gonna punch your face off!

September 28, 2025: I wish we could talk to the humans. Seems like a lot going on down there. Did you eat the last Glory bar? I hate you so much.

October 31, 2025, 10:43 AM: Uh-oh. I think Mom found us. We are so grounded.

I can only imagine how people would behave if a spacecraft appeared in our atmosphere. I fervently hope this imagining is wrong.

Without Her

I shift, restless
In my comfy chair
My favorite drink
Right next to my seat
A fire burning bright
To ward off the chill of night
But there is no comfort
Here or anywhere
The ice softly clinks
As confined as I and
Dying just the same
A weary sigh escapes
My mind sees her smile
Hears her laughing, even
With me by the fire
Flames dancing merrily in her eyes
But the mind is a cruel
Despicable thing
The delusion refuses to hold
There is no warmth
From the glowing coals
And I am unbearably cold
For without her
It's merely a light show
The hearth may just as well
Be filled with snow
The wind outside blows
Somehow whistling viciously
Through my soul
Reminding me that
I'm alone
Alone, isolated, bereft
An empty bottle
With no spirits left
But then I think
Must this be it?
Is there no other way?
Am I to become this?
This broken down, pathetic wretch
All because *she* left?
Suddenly I became enraged
My voice rose in my chest
I sprang from my seat
In the greatest of protest

Filled with contempt
I wept, I rallied, I cried
I profaned her name
I smashed her picture
In its frame
I crushed my glass to death!
And after all of that
After I'd spent
What little fire I had left
The damnable answer
Was still yes
Deflated, I poke the coals
Wishing she were sitting there
So I could again stare
Upon her ebon hair
I long for her to know
Deep in her elegant soul
That I loved her so
But merely couldn't show it
That the loss of her
Makes me less
That the mistakes I made
Haunt me each day
That I will sit here, broken
Unable to go
Until every single spark of life
Is choked from this home
Including my own

Trudging through the airport, past tired, grouchy, hungry, wanting to be home. Then I saw this dude. Jacket off, tie loosened, hair askew, red-rimmed eyes. A glass of something amber sat in front of him (it all sounds so cliché). He alternated between twisting his wedding band and staring down at his phone. This is his fault.

What's not his fault are the eight freaking versions of this. We're not talking about it.

On a side note, I think I was born in the wrong era. I can't imagine how delighted I would be to tell someone "Verily, an it doth please thee, go forth past yonder breach and fucketh thyself most vigorously, providing no means of lubrication, until thy very death, Sir." Then slap dude with a glove?

WHEE! If you don't pee a little over excitement at that, I'm not sure we can be friends.

Oh Toronto

Late night, Toronto
Frosty, dark and sparkling
I'm walking down Yonge Street
Taking in the sights
Breathing the chill December air
Going wherever my face takes me
Enjoying this city's life
Having the grandest time
Until another's eyes meet mine
They hold me there
I can't pull away
The mini-skirt and faux fur
Keep out nothing of the cold
Yet offer me an open window
Into all of their hoping
That someone, anyone
Is as lonely as I think they must be
That the cold
Comes only from the outside
That it has no hold
That a warm body
Will thaw a frozen space
Which I know can't be reached
By peddling themselves on the street
So I ask
Hot chocolate or coffee?
Room for cream?
Fluffy marshmallows?
There's this place nearby with great
Espresso and pecan cookies
They stare at me, shocked
Don't speak
They're gauging, wondering
Am I'm predator or prey?
I shrug, walk away
And return with the treats
I just grabbed a variety of things
Their surprise was delightful
I thought I saw a brightness
Inside their gray sky eyes
But then they blinked
Iron bars on windowpanes
Shutters locked down tight
Curtains closed

Oh Toronto!
Even when you're ugly
I love you so

I saw a trans sex worker in Toronto one evening. It was horribly cold outside. I wanted to buy them coffee, or tea, or anything. Truth is, I didn't have the courage to approach. I didn't want them to think I was interested in anything other than providing a warm drink. Not predator. Not prey.

Random: Hi Trevor Noah! Love you, love your show.

Suspicious

Your suspicious ears
Don't hear
Truthful news
Your closed heart
Can't receive
Adoring gifts
Your bitter tongue
Won't taste
Devoted love
And you
Are a fucking idiot!

I think I dated the most suspicious minded dude in this galaxy. Everything was turned into something else.

Everything. That shit wore me dafuq out. I got so tired of explaining things THAT WEREN'T EVEN THINGS. No, I don't model to get attention from other men so I can leave you. No, I didn't hug my cousin to make you jealous. No, I didn't set my alarm early so I could go fuck someone else. Goodness.

It doesn't matter what you do. People like that find a way to warp the most innocuous occurrence into something heinous, sneaky, deceitful, dirty, pick your word. I got to a point where I stopped explaining and started adding fuel to the fire. It was gotdamn childish, but somewhere in there I got fukkin' mad. Let's do some petty shit, mad. YAY!

At the end, I realized how stupid I was being. I'ontevenknow how or why I let it get that far or go on for so long. UGH.

But have you noticed that people like that are always above reproach? Lousy fuckers.

Neon green jacket
Sunshine smile
A merry wave
Though it's not for me
I take it personally
My day is made
Thank you lady crossing guard!

I see a school crossing guard on my way to work. She's tiny, wizened, and missing a bunch of teeth. But GAWD, does she smile like she doesn't have a single care in the universe! I know she's not smiling for me, but I choose to believe she is anyway. I like it. A LOT.

Perspective

March 23, 2015
Her: I tilt my face up to his kiss. It's blustery outside according to the moron who delivered the weather report. I shiver as his lips press mine. I look away. He chuckles, asks if I'm cold. Really? It's four fucking degrees outside. *Am I cold?* No asshole, I'm shivering with delight. I'm thinking of shoving a knife down his throat.

Maybe tonight I will. He's ripe for the picking as they say. He trusts me completely. But I've had enough of his reptile lips, his stupid hair, his ridiculous clothes and his braying donkey laugh. I'm tired of his lumpy form next to me in bed. Tired of his dumb jokes. Tired of his inept hands. I'm fucking tired of *him.*

Him: She tilts her face up to my kiss. Lips warm, despite the blustery day. She shivers when my lips press hers. She looks away. I know she's cold but ask anyway. It's four fucking degrees outside. I'm a moron. I know the shiver isn't delight. She hates me. She thinks of killing me multiple time a day. Will tonight be the night? She wields those knives like a Samurai. She's smart. She could make it look like an accident. I know this and yet I can't get enough of her soft lips, her beautiful hair, her stylish clothes, her musical laugh. I love her curvy form next to me in bed. Her brilliant jokes.

Her skilled hands. I'm so in love with her.

March 23, 2019
Her: I can't believe it. Four years together. We made it! He's worked so hard. He's done everything I wanted. What a complete turnaround! It's just amazing. All my friends are jealous. It's perfect. HE'S PERFECT!

Him: Bitch dies tonight. Four years of bullshit. Dancing to her stupid little tune. Like some kind of fucking puppet.

What a stupid cow. I'll make it look like an accident. FUCK. HER.

I see so many couples fight, break up, get back together. Wash. Rinse. Repeat. I imagine thoughts like these aren't too far off in some of those relationships. That thin line, you know?

Have you ever been with someone you knew was stupid for you, but you went for it anyway? Did you think red flag city was the circus? It was. Full of clowns.

Don't lie to me. Or yourself. That's how you ended up in that relationship, just like this one, back in '86, which should have been over in five minutes, but instead, three years later, you're plotting a way to kill the asshole in their sleep.

Poison

Words more poison
Than spider's venom
Drip
Down your rotten tongue
Tighter and tighter
You weave and wind
A web of deceit
A spate of lies
Injection, infection
Confusion, paralysis
Death
The unwary, unwise
And too hopeful
Have no hope
Against you
Your intent to sow dissent
Propagate strife
Is fully realized
How delighted
You must be
To ply your craft
But in this house
Poison spiders
Are crushed flat
Legs broken; guts busted
Put out with the trash

Supposedly grown folks spend entirely too much time playing games, trying to be slick, being hateful, conniving, creating drama. And to what end? Is there a point somewhere? I don't have the time or inclination to deal with that kind of juvenile bullshit.

Like my mama bear says, I'll pass you like Christ passed Cicero.

FYI: If you are constantly embroiled in something and always at the center of controversy? Common denominator, baby. The problem is most likely you. Go cut yourself on Occam's Razor.

Daybreak

Open my eyes
And I am greeted
By peach and coral ribbons
Outside my window
I watch the golden sun
Chart a path to my tired face
In a slowly brightening sky
Dreams I was dreaming, fade
While I breathe in the warmth
Of a coming day and sigh
I hear a bluebird trilling
And spare a moment of pity
My old gray owl needs his sleep!
But that is no more for me
I slip silently through the house
Enjoying the groans it makes
As I navigate
Through the still dark space
To where the green kettle waits
On a battered silver stove
I sit at my oaken table
In a faded yellow kitchen
Filled with hope

I used to have a big oaken table in a retro yellow kitchen. I loved it so much. This thing kinda wrote itself.

I will tell you, I am not a girl for the morning. But! I wake up every day grateful for the chance to try again. To make better choices, be kinder, be happier, be healthier, hell, to just be above ground. The gift of a new day is something we too often take for granted.

Don't let me lie, though. Some days I wake up Crusty T. McBitchface. I'm still grateful, I'm just a bitch about it.

Memory Tree

Do you remember?
When we used to meet
To read our comics
Or share a treat
Beneath that ratty old tree
At the end of our street
Dear Lord,
It looked diseased!
With its scarred-up trunk
And crunchy brown leaves
We measured our heights
Against its body
We shared our hearts
Among its roots
We spoke of what we'd do
When we grew
We'd even sneak a kiss or two
Not knowing what it meant
The only things that worried us
Were creatures scurrying under us
Picking at our legs through the grass
Or the squirrel that used to harass
Chittering and chattering his tirade
Oh, how we'd laugh!
Then one day our tree was gone
Uprooted from its place
By a man with a hateful face
"Find somewhere else to play!"
He raged, we vowed revenge
We wished him zits and smelly feet
As there was truly nothing else
Two gangly kids could do
Our lives changed that day
Our idyll, broken
Never to be regained
Now we have children of our own
Responsibilities to things
Some we don't want or need
And so sometimes I cling
To our memories
They cover and comfort
When the world makes no sense
The blue sky, the brilliant sun
Young love and innocence

Fearlessness and freedom
And the truth?
The place in my heart
Where you live
Will forever and lovingly be tended
No matter what else I do
Nothing will compare
To the lifetime we shared
Just you and me
Beneath that ratty old tree

Good childhood memories are such treasures. Sometimes the drudgery and pressure of adulthood make us long for those days. Just me? Oh, okay.

This is a piece of wishful thinking. I never had a little boy friend or boyfriend. I never snuck a kiss and didn't know enough to know I wanted to. I read my comics alone under the tree. I was a quiet, solo, nerdy little girl with long skinny arms and legs, knobby little knees, and tangled hair. My glasses were thick.

I grew into a nerdy adult, with long arms and legs and tangled hair. These days there might be a boy somewhere who wants to kiss me. Might be.

The Trees of My Childhood

The trees of my childhood have gnarled bark, dark leaves
They wave their branches at me: What did you do?
Why did you leave? Who are you?
I cringe beneath their accusations—head bowed, unworthy
When I was a child, I knew them all! But now?
I am a woman grown, no scraped-up knees
No respect for the sacrifice of trees
With a sickness hovering, hovering
On a tongue grown dull from grown up conversation
And no more secrets to share
I am rattled and bereaved; I am dying
I long for tall grass and raspberries
I long to wake from this sleep
Where I've lost the love of trees

After a poem by Edith Södergran. This was another assignment I think I misunderstood. I got an A, but I wonder if it even sounds like me. Weird. I fall into these spaces where I don't make sense to myself. Stranger's hand again, I suppose.

Star Wars

Star Wars! I fell in love at a young age and refuse to give it up. My kitchen could double as a cantina for the aliens. The shelves in my office are full of Funkos. I have Wookiee pajamas. Star Wars chopsticks. A droid herb grinder. No, not that kind. T-shirts, hoodies, aprons, socks, mugs.

Magnets. Cookie cutters. Prints. Coloring books. You get it. Princess Leia was my first girl crush. RIP Carrie Fisher.

Thank you Jon Favreau for The Mandalorian, but if something bad happens to Grogu? I will Liam Neeson you. That's *mostly* a joke.

This abruptly brings me to gate keepers. So many times, when I've been wearing one of my Star Wars t-shirts, some dude, yes always a dude, felt the need to grill me on Star Wars. Several years ago, a guy on a coffee date asked me if I knew what happened to Boba Fett. I said "No, but I know I never want to talk to you again." That was a lie. Of course, I know what happened to Boba Fett.

Same with almost every artist tee I wear. I had on a Kill Em All shirt once (yup, love Metallica too), and this douche canoe challenged me to name any song off the album. I told him I was certain Cliff Burton wasn't paying him to verify my fan status. He said, "Who is Cliff Burton?" Fuckhead.

FYI: This is incredibly rude, and it's not your business what level of fan anyone is or even if they actually are a fan. Why do you fucking care? Do you enjoy being a smug asshole? FOHRFN. If that's how you flirt, go back to Tips on Being a Man. Chapter 3, Don't Be a Douche! Effective Ways to Flirt.

Being a fan doesn't mean you have to know what Djimon Honsou eats (Mr. Honsou, I remember the first time I saw you!) or what day does Denzel Washington his laundry (Swoon, Mr. Washington!). Leave people alone. Or just me. It won't end well for you anyway, so I'm trying to be nicer than you deserve. Don't make me John Wick you. (Mr. Reeves—YUM! But I do wish I had half your calm reservoir.)

Waiting

From skinned knees
And climbing trees
To driving and graduation
Life events you missed
No phone call or letter
To prove you exist
Or even have an interest
In a pensive young woman
Carrying your smile on her face
Who often acts like you
To her mother's dismay
You gave me life
But kept your heart away
I pretend that I'm okay
That my own heart doesn't ache
That the woman
I am now
Is over skinned knees and trees
And the father she's never seen
I pretend the thoughts don't creep
Wear me down, make me weep
That tears don't flow
In a rush out of my soul
That your absence didn't affect
That I scorned your neglect
Even the feel of your anger
Would have been a gift
But what did you give?
A big spoonful of nothing
To complete the empty set
And what about you, Dad
Should I even call you that?
Do you ever think about me?
Care to see what you created?
On the hot August day I arrived
Did I fill you with pride
Even for a moment?
My soul says otherwise
Do you know I almost died?
Would you have faltered
If I was gone from this place?
Would I finally matter to you?
Would you have cried?
Do you know that I loved you

Though you never came?
Do you care that I'm still here
After all these years
Hating myself for waiting?

No explanation needed right? This whole thing taught me that I don't need closure. From anyone. EV-ER.

About anything. You don't want to talk to me? Don't. Want to break up? Please do. I don't want or need to hear whatever cooked up bullshit story you need to make yourself feel better. Fuck outta here. And I say that smiling. I'm not even mad.

It's up to me, the decisions. About what to feel, how to think, how to process. Why should anyone else's input factor?

And please pray tell me, why we give people power over us that don't deserve it? Why do we seek approval, attention and affection from those hell bent on NOT giving it to us? What is this ailment called? Is there an ointment for it? Lobotomy! It's a lobotomy, isn't it? I was afraid you'd say that.

PS: I did attempt/am attempting to find another half-brother. More for health information than anything. Or maybe that's what I tell myself.

Speaking of Dating... Nice Segue, Huh?

Before I moved to AZ, I went on a ridiculous number of dates. Ridiculous! The most I would usually commit to was coffee, but there were a few dinners. I chose coffee because it's short. If I didn't like dude, I didn't waste too much time. I wasn't looking to eat. I cook for myself thanks. I'm not a drinker so coffee it was.

I posted about the dates on a dedicated Facebook page—Dickpicks and Misadventures. I wanted to try something different, so I did this through online dating. I thought it would be fun. GAWD. I wish someone had punched me in the porta hepatis because that would have sucked a fuck of a lot less. I ended up hating this more than I thought possible. I couldn't keep up with where I was with whomever it was, I was talking to. The mistakes were EPIC. Some were funny, but mostly it was awful.

I did have the presence of mind to get one of those dummy phone lines. It saved me.

Cooper's Squawk

Setting is dinner at Cooper's Hawk. I'm 5'9 today. Wait. I'm that height every day.

I walk in and this guy looks up at me. He approaches looking frowny and confused.

Him: Aristah? Wow, you're much taller than I thought you'd be.

He pronounced my name wrong. Like Air-is-duh. Fuck.

Me (laughing): Yeah. It's Aristah. How tall did you think 5'9 was?
Him: What? What do you mean?
The way he said it was A-NOY-YING. Yes, I know there's another N.
Me (staring muthafuckily): Are you kidding? My profile says I'm 5'9.
Him (still confused): What? Oh well. I just didn't know you'd be this big.
Me (utterly fucking astounded): Big?
Mind, we're in the foyer whispering and it's a Herculean effort not to be a bitch.
Him: What?
Me: Hey pal, I think this is a bad idea. You obviously have an issue with my height.

Can you believe I called him pal? How old am I?

Him (gaping like a moron): What? You think you're too tall for me?
Samuel L. Jackson is in my head losing his cool (I love him too. Hi Mr. Jackson!) Say what again! I dare you. I double dare you, motherfucker! Folks! I am thinking evil things. EVIL.
Him: You're way out of my league anyway. I didn't even think you'd show up.

WTMFF FYYFF EABOSD YFAC (what the motherfuckin fuck, fuck you, you fucking fuck, eat a bag of salted dicks, you fucking ass clown).

Me: You're right, I **am absolutely** out of **your** league.

I walked out. Went to the bookstore. Got a giant cookie. He left a million apologies on my fake phone. NOPE.

Ok penis owners. Two things. One: If YOU have an issue with a woman's height don't make HER feel bad about it. Just don't ask her out. Is that hard? Why are y'all fucking this up?

I will admit, I used to have this thing about only dating very tall men. But guess what? That was my own insecurity about my height coupled with encounters like this. We'll talk about it in a minute.

Two: What is this league shit? Put that trash back in stupid pocket. Stupid pocket is an area of your brain, btw.

To be fair, there are a couple of camps here. Camp 1: The dudes who truly think that woman is otherworldly. They love her, cherish her, and treat her like a goddess. They're grateful to have her. They work to get where they think she is. We like these dudes.

Camp 2: Filled with manipulative assholes who use it like a compliment. Hoping we reverse psyche ourselves and get all drippy because you think so highly of us, we just have to give you a chance. GTFOH bruh. We not fallin' fuh dat no mo. We immensely disklike this dude. He gets a throat punch or ten.

But fellas, if you truly thought a woman was out of your league, why were you messing with her? Wasting her time? It's an excuse to be a lazy piece of shit is what it is. You can't be blamed for half-assing and fucking up everything because poor wittle you is oh so confused about what to do with such a woman. Let me help you out. LEAVE HER THE FUCK ALONE.

Same goes for you ladies too. Though if I catch oneay'all doing this, we havin' words. Unfriendly words.

Now, I'm only 5'9. Not super tall, but I'm all limbs. Long fingers, 34.5" inseam, long arms, size 10 shoe. The only wanting very tall men thing? I never felt safe. I wanted to be protected by a man. STEWPID. There is no correlation. I know tall guys who are weak as wet tissue (character wise and physically) and short guys who could mow down six tall dudes, laugh the whole time, bring you flowers, and not break a sweat.

I should have been smart and looked for someone who would protect my heart. Instead, I developed strong feelings for weak men just because they were TALL. Read it again. I did this shit to myself.

Tall or short. Black or white. Skinny or fat. Rich or poor. The wrong man is the wrong man. He'll disappoint you, hurt you, and aggravate you to no end. The right man will do quite the opposite.

The other part is you asshole penis owners. "You're so big." Pardon me? Tall does not equal big. Tall is tall. Or "Do you have to wear heels?" Yeah motherfucker, I do!

This is very easy.

If you don't like my height, don't get in line for the ride!

Wilted

Welp! You'll be surprised to hear that I was dating a guy I shouldn't have been. Very tall, very handsome, very well off, very controlling. At first, it looked like care. He was worried about me. Wanted to make sure I was safe. That I had the best. It was all for me. You can smell the bullshit from wherever you are, can't you? I was already struggling a bit with all his *caring* when this happened. Mind, this was only three months into things.

Let's call him Tom. Tom wants me to attend a black-tie event in a few weeks. He's beyond excited. Now, even though I consistently suck in matters of the heart this bitch knows how to dress. Leather, lace, silk, satin, cotton, gabardine, burlap. You get the point. Anyway, Tom tells me he has a surprise coming for me. Who doesn't love surprises?

A box I would have fit in arrives at my place. Inside the box is a dress. Shoes. Purse. Jewelry. From Saks. Which would have been great except for the color, style, and length of said dress. I'm a size 2 at this point of my life and this dress is huge, honkin', ginormous, big. Folds, fluff, puffs, bows and fuckery. This thing had a ruffle from throat to twat. It's also a petite dress, so it's BIG and SHORT! I'm 5'9! I haven't been considered petite since I was seven years old. When I tell you the color was old iceberg lettuce with wilted edges, I'm being extremely polite. It's a color *I know* makes me look like I'm about to embark on a festival of violent, soul ripping, projectile puking due to a month long bender. I'm figuring out the nicest way to break this to Tom when he arrives. This has been a while, so the convo isn't verbatim but pretty close.

Tom: I see the dress came. It's much better in person.

Me: I'm a little worried about the color. Why don't I try it on for you?

Tom says something asinine about being happy to get a sneak peek but he's sure it will look amazing. In my head, I'm wondering if he's suffering temporary blindness, but whatever. I know once he sees it, he'll realize how awful it is.

I go and put the contraption on. I am HORRIFIED. HORRRRRRIIIIIIIFIED. Forget the bender. I'm on the table getting my stomach pumped and a step from death. The pink curtain is nearly exposed, the arm holes are somehow tight despite how fucking big this thing is, and that ruffle is obscene. There is also some kind of scaly sheen to it. I mean, BLECH.

I walk out, and to my ultimate horror, Tom says he loves the dress.

Me (confused): You're kidding. There is no way I can wear this. It's too—

Tom: No. You are absolutely wearing that dress. Do you know how much it cost? Do you know how much time I spent looking for it?

Me: I appreciate the effort, I really do. But—

Tom: Stop this right now. You are going to wear it.

Me: No. I have a closet full of dresses that—

Tom: Yes. You are. Wearing it.

Me: I absolutely am not.

Tom: We are not arguing about this.

Me: You're right. I'm—

Tom: Good girl.

Me:

Tom starts rambling on about how much fun the event is going to be while failing to realize I have steam coming out of the top of my head, eyes are mere slits, and the nostrils are on 70s flare.

Me (annoyed now and speaking very slowly): Tom, I'm not wearing that dress. I don't care how long it took to find. I don't care how much it cost.

Tom starts yelling at me about how ungrateful I am. I was barely listening or moving. He manages to insert a "Do you know how many women want to be in your shoes?"

Me (almost growling): Again, you're right. Go get one of *those* women and put **HER** in that ugly fucking lettuce dress. Take the jewelry, the shoes and that stupid purse and shove them in your dick hole (this was the first time I'd used dick hole threateningly—very effective).

Tom (after a long silence): You know. I was going to buy you a car for your birthday.

Me: I can buy my own car, Tom. You can shove that car in your asshole if you choose. I don't want or need anything from you except for you to leave.

Tom: We will talk about this tomorrow when *you* are more rational.

I am on fire. I'm so mad I can't see, and I know I'm about to lose it. I tell Tom to wait. I go box up every gift given to me over the three months. Bracelets, earrings, a necklace, a ring, a watch. All expensive.

I handed the box to Tom and told him there was nothing to discuss. I wished him luck with the dress and his future and opened the door. He was shook, shocked, and all kinds of pissed off.

Tom called me every single day, multiple times a day, for weeks. Telling me I had made a mistake. That I would be sorry. That I needed someone like him to take care of me. Tom fetishized me. He wanted to show off his new shiny skinny GASP black girlfriend. He had never dated a black woman. He used me as his trial. Didn't want to go all the way, THAT'S CRAZY! Light skin for the win! (BARF) He wanted a little doll he could dress up and play with, that he thought he could control. What a jackass.

For once, I figured it out early and saved myself. Yay me. If only I had been that smart all the time. Nope. UGH.

FYI: If you're ever arguing with me and I start whispering, leave the state. Do NOT tell *anybody* where you're going. Why? Cuz I'm actively trying to figure out how to avoid capture for viciously brutalizing the corpse I'm about to create.

And PS: I find it extremely sexy to let a man dress me. But! He does have to know what the hell he's doing.

Sumay'all need help. A lot of help.

Sleep

Dear Sleep,
Could we speak?
Have a conversation
A meeting of minds
I need to find out
Why you left me
We used to be so close
Spending every night together
And some pleasant afternoons
I loved cuddling with you
Now you're nowhere to be found
I need you around
My arms are empty
Will you ever come back?
I'll do anything you ask
Even that one thing
Me, face down
Mouth agape and drooling
Come on, Sleep
Don't do me like this
I really miss you
I'm begging
Sleep?
Sleep? You there?
Please?

I have these bouts of insomnia. Nothing works. One night I took two Ambien and stayed up for hours after. What kind of fuckery is that?

I get pretty desperate for sleep. I mean, this is brutal. I get loopy and all kinds of weird. It honestly makes me stupid. So, if I'm being a dummy, I'm probably supercalafragafuckingtired.

Anyone else? What do you do?

Consume

The moment I see her
I know that she's mine
I watch
As the light dims
Behind her eyes
I feel her
Yearning toward me
She leans so closely
To hear me speak
Her adoration
Is devastating, brimming over
But she is starving
She desires
To devour *me*
Snuff out my flame
I cannot allow her
To tame me
Yet if I spurn her
I fear she might break
This way I can make her
Do whatever I say
No resistance will she offer
To anything I proffer
I can take my time
Hide inside
I can see, smell, touch
Lick, if I wish
Twist my fingers
Breathe her in
Consume her
By the inch
Bend her over
Until she tips
Drunken and sated
Into dawn

THIS is not about THAT. I warned you at the beginning. You decide what it's about. Write me. Tell me your thoughts. I'm curious.

And hey, sometimes I wake up with a wild hair. Right. All of mine are wild, but I mean the brain hair. Wait. There's no brain hair. You know what I'm saying! I have to get that hair picked or plucked or I will go crazy(er). And you, my dear reader, end up sitting there like you are right now wondering what I ate or what the heck I was doing to inspire such.

Question that isn't a question: Can we talk about Stephen King? I love him. Always have. It's creepy level love. Not nearly as creepy as some of the shit he writes, but dang! I remember begging my mama bear to let me read his books when I was too young. She let me because SHE IS AWESOME. I remember I put *The Shining* in the freezer because I was so scared of it. What the hell was the freezer gonna do? I still don't know, but maybe I thought it would calm the hellfire coming out of that damn book.

Stephen, umm, Mr. King, if you ever see this, I LOVE YOU! Thank you so much for scaring the ever-loving fuck out of little me.

If you're sitting there passing judgment on my mother, stop right now. She knows me. You do not. She was there.

Books soothed a lot of hurts and let me escape. She realized that and I love her even more for it.

Puffy clouds above
Misty fog below
The mountains enthrall
I can't stop staring
My mind imagines a doorway
To another place
Where my heart is light
And my soul is whole
A place to sleep
That the demons can't reach
Where I give myself
To its cotton candy embrace
And I am accepted

The mountains here absolutely entrance me. Naked, covered in fog, their tops dusted with snow. It doesn't matter. I see them and imagination takes over. It's always somewhere magical and calm. As stated, a place of acceptance.
I do worry that one day I will wreck my car, but that's on me.

War

(Warning: The below entry is terrible IMO, but its story is cute)

The sun shines
Upon the sea
But not upon this land
Not upon me
Black rain falls
In the heaviest sheet
Immersing
Submerging
Drowning
Complete
Chaos rules this land
Dark hearts hold sway
Kindness costs a fortune
I cannot afford to pay
Red fires rage
With the brightest heat
Feeding
Spreading
Burning
Deceit
Flows purposely on the air
Friends are foes, lovers hate
Misdirection is the fare
Served on a frozen plate
White winds roar
Abundantly filled with sleet
Blasting
Tearing
Ripping
Meat
Slashed from enemy bones
My passion starts to fade
Fighting a stranger's war
Not worth my soul in trade
Silver swords fly
Cutting
Stabbing
Ending
Defeat
Rings out of the fray

For whom we cannot know
Our blood spills the same
Staining the pristine snow
Obsolete

War (Alternate)

The sun is weak
And can barely peek
Through the black rain
Falling in heavy sheets
Immersing us, submerging us,
Drowning us
Complete chaos rules our land
Dark hearts hold sway
Kindness costs a fortune
I cannot afford to pay
The war bringer has taken his fee
And left me empty
Deceit flows heavily in the air
Friends are foes, lovers hate
Misdirection is the fare
Served on a frozen plate
I beg for the rain to end
Only to be given red fires
Raging with the brightest heat
Burning us, destroying us,
Consuming us
The war bringer has taken our meat
And left us hungry
Come with me to war, he said
And I will bring you glory
And so, we followed
But we were never told
We'd give our souls in trade
That silver swords would fly
That our people would die
The war bringer has taken our lives
And left us with nothing
Except defeat
Ringing out of the fray
For them or us, I don't know
Our blood spills the same
Staining the pristine snow
The golden angels cry

My imagination is twisted. I was looking at an old, super cool, broken chess set in a tiny shop, in New Jersey/Pennsylvania. For some reason, the pawn told me he was tired of the game and couldn't take it any longer. He wanted out so I bought him. He became a gift to someone and I hope he's no longer at war. Yeah, I know—CRAZY.

But! I'm glad my imagination goes wild. I play with the visions that invade. Some days the reptile in there worries me, but mostly I'm delighted by the child.

PS: I never got this to be what I wanted. There are 13 versions. 13! I told you it was kinda bad. I don't even think these two are the best. I put it in here because it's a total fail and sometimes sharing failure lessens it for me. I could give you guys a whole BOOK full of failures.

Do you feel lucky yet?

Cliché

tick tock
tick tock
goes the cliché clock
driving me to violence
warping my brain
killing all forethought
with the inane
mundane and reclaimed
imagery uninspired
has replaced
imagination
this is crime!
we must find
something
much more
unexpected
to say
find
some other way
to convey
what goes on
in the front
back and sides
of our expansive
minds
let us create
a literary storm
rain down our
genius
like it's the norm
our typical
form
prove
our mastery
in this art of words
leave the
impostors
lonely and lost
let them not
build
their dull dynasty
on the ashes
of our
luminosity

let us
crush
mediocrity
while we dance
and play
bend them
make them break
until they beg
for just
the barest sip
of the silken
nectar of
intelligence
flowing so
abundantly
from our able
lips

I got nothin for ya here. NOTHIN. I was simply sitting there, annoying my dog most likely, and this came out of my face. Most of the time, that's how I 'write'.

Grave Clothes

I've been walking the streets
In my grave clothes
I've not been discreet
The natives are shirking
Turning up their noses
As if they discern an odor
Yet the modest bird
Who lit upon my shoulder
Chirp, chirped and dug in
With his black taloned feet
His nares did not flare
As I don't think he cares
My cerements are to his liking
He himself is dark, so dark
Like the corners of Observatory Park
And his eyes are as bright
As Canopus at night
But the further we traipse
From light and invention
The more I become lost
In him, my traveling attendant
Who is quite the puzzlement
Of soothing and Grimm
It occurs to me then
To be leery of his attention
My mind attempts to rail
My body fails to listen
Not a shrug or shudder
Could I muster
Then this bird
With his talons in my shirt
Turns his beak as if to speak
Not a word did he utter
But I heard him!
His sable silk wings
Cut into my cheek
It's then I know
This is *not*
The fabled raven of Poe's
But a bird, bleaker still
Sent to cull me
From my carbon hull
Excuse me bird!
I WILL NOT GO!

I will rage and fight!
My light will not die!
And then this bird, this bird
With his talons in my shirt
Chortled!
Poor child, said he
No need to fight so violently
I merely came
To walk you home
So you wouldn't be alone

Ode to Poe and Thomas

Zero idea what happens when we die. It would be cool to have an escort, though. Except...

I don't like birds. But I do. Could I be any more confusing? I hate birds chirping in the morning. I hate pigeons. I always think they're plotting. Geese are not from here and I wish they'd go the fuck back home.

Rude. Ass. Creeps.

Hummingbirds are cool AF and I like ducks. Ravens and crows are amazing. I enjoy watching predator birds swoop, soar, and dive. And of course, I love my savior bird. You'll meet her later. Yeah, I could have just said I like birds except for geese and pigeons. Fuck them.

What's Your Fantasy?

Dude—I won't say man because he wasn't—I was dating asked me what kind of fantasies I had and what my body count was. We had not yet bumped uglies, and I saw no harm in telling him at least one fantasy and my low body count. I mean, I think asking body count is juvenile but whatever.

This fucking clown proceeded to let me know how horrified (clutch those pearls!) he was by my body count, and how perverse he thought my fantasy was. How I needed to get right with God and reevaluate my existence. I proceeded to let him know he needed to go the *fuckhome,* one word, and *forget* about *my* existence.

Now, I did not say one thing about bestiality, necrophilia, BDSM, midgets, fisting, feet, fluids, other people, or even light spanking. Nothing crazy, promise.

It hurt. Made me mad. Made me hesitate to share with anyone else.

Fellas—DO NOT. This is way worse than sending an unsolicited dick pic. Just don't. And here's a sidebar…

Dudes of the Universe

I can't believe I even have to write this, but DO NOT SEND AN UNSOLICITED DICK PIC. DO NOT. STOP. NO. DON'T. NO. NO. NO. NO. NO. NO. NO. NO. NO. NO. NO.

NO. And guess what else? NO. NOPE. Unh-unh. NOOOOOOO.

Do you know how many plucked chicken bits I've had to hurriedly delete? It's appalling. Even if we ASK for one, make us sign a form stating that we did indeed ask for said picture of said dick. Maybe have it signed in blood. Make sure it's dated. Put an expiration on it.

Now, back to the story. Please don't be the guy who treats his woman to missionary only and does all the 'perverse' things with someone else out of some supposed respect. That's trash and you know it.

Ladies, you already know not to do this, right? If you need a refresher on fantasy rules, I believe it's on page 93, paragraph four, sentence two of "A Peek Behind the Pink Curtain".

And sorry, if you're stuck on body count, go get your insecurities checked. That's a lie. I'm not sorry. I think you're ridiculous. You're afraid someone before you did it better.

That she's dreaming of him while you're hittin' on nothin' but your own ego. I'm using dudes, but it goes both ways.

Don't act like you're worried about health! If so, ask the real question:

"When was the last time you had an STI check? If it's been a while, can we go together?"

But you're not doing that. You'd rather slut shame. Go fuck *yourself* with that.

Is Ludacris in your head now? Haha if he is.

Still

Hold very still
They said
Just a slight pinch
Might burn a bit
And something that feels
Like a stitch
A sewing machine
If you will
Inside your chest
HA!
The burn was an inferno
That stitch was a bitch
My neck feels broken
Sitting here all twisted
When I realize
They never said
What could happen
In my heart or head
That for a moment
My ability to speak
Would leave
That sorrow might overtake
That dread would threaten
Weaken my spine
That for a time
I might feel so afraid
I wanted to cry
That my strength and courage
Were a well already run dry
They never said
But I know
I just have to hold very still

Can't Fly

Stuck in Superman
But I'm not him
I can't fly!
I don't have a penis!
Arms high
Above my head
For an MRI
On this fucking
Uncomfortable bed
Breasts laid bare
Not going anywhere
There's an IV in me
These stupid pads
Are definitely not rad
Face smashed into a shape
That makes me think
Of a urinal cake
Ugh! Great!
Spa music plays
Doing nothing to allay
The things I'm feeling
Finally
After a near eternity
A voice comes on
Good job! You're almost done
I sigh at the lie
As my journey
Has just begun

The Wire

Palms are sweaty
But there's no vomit
Or Mom's spaghetti
Wait!
That's Em's line
Mine?
Been NPO since nine
No food, no drink
Not even a chip of ice
My throat is stupid dry
I'm back on the table
This time for a wire
Not the kind for birds
Or the kind David likes
This isn't homicide
Except maybe for my spirit
The biopsy Aussie is back too
He's here for the stick
I'm Superman again
It's so unpleasant
The needle goes in
I grit my teeth, clench
More sweat beads
I feel the wire
Inside me, an alien thing
I don't want it
But there's no choice
Not in any of this
The machine grinds
Its coils spinning
Taking pictures of me
I'm not smiling

Partial-ly

Dr. V
Took a little bit
More of me
It's for the best
And perhaps this
Will be it
No need
To take the rest
In this case
Partial is preferred
But if that's a no
These blobs of flesh
Can go
They aren't me
I'm not them
Whether they're here or not
I am whole

Steri-Strips

There's Steri-Strips
On my TTs
White striped
And sticky
Covering
The upside down
Smile, cut
Over my nips
Scars above
Scars below
No scars inside though
No shower for 48 hours
Which stinks
I likely will too
This pink bra thing
Is a snug
Boa hugging me
And I think
I really think
I deserve cookies
I'm sleepy

If you can't tell, Curly Girl had a bad mammo. Atypical ductal hyperplasia + family history = a high-risk number. Biopsy. MRI. Genetic test. Consultation. Surgery planning. That dirty M-word. The even dirtier C-word. Scary.

My experience with all of it was mild compared to many, but still.

There was a point in the biopsy where I froze. I was joking with the radiologist when everything locked up. My voice broke and stopped. My brain stuttered. I was gripped by stillness. I couldn't even blink. You know that nightmare paralysis? All me. The nurse rubbed my back and kept soothing me. She'd seen it before, she knew. I loved her right then. When the paralysis passed, I had a second where I wanted to jump up and run from the chair. From the office. From my own skin. Fuck. Then I went back to jokes because I didn't have anything else.

The still thing is twofold. Sometimes when you're still, clarity comes. Sometimes when you're still it's out of fear. This still was not the clarity type. There's absolutely nothing you can do about it either. Well, except hold still.

I thought I was prepared for an onslaught of emotions during all this. Haha. DUMB. I'm looking down at the steri-strips one day and decide they're the man holding my nipples down. Those fargin iceholes! (Ode to Johnny Dangerously) How rude! We had to hatch an escape! I started to laugh and couldn't stop. Then I was crying and couldn't stop.

That same day my oldest brother sent me a fruit bouquet (Umm, who knew chocolate-covered pineapple was good and didn't tell me? Jerks!) with a sweet card and an I Love You balloon. Crying. I was off most of that afternoon. No more crying just off. It shocked me. It shouldn't have. Silver lining? I found out I don't like the taste of chocolate and tears together.

But you know what I really wasn't prepared for? The blankness I felt. Don't let me lie to you. I had moments of crushing terror, sadness, fear. But they faded. The blankness for real fucked me up. I don't know if it was a protection mechanism or denial or what, but it was weird AF. I need to unpack all this one day when I'm up to it. Not today. And 100% not tomorrow.

I know how much worse this could have been for me. My warrior woman mama bear is a 33-year survivor! Maybe that was part of it? I know how lucky I am. I'm grateful to be here.

Side note: If you've ever had an MRI, Superman position sucks. If you've ever had an MRI in Superman position with your boobs loose, that sucks worse.

'Homicide: A Year on the Killing Streets' by David Simon is one of my favorite books ever and I also loved 'The Wire'. Omar, sadly, is no longer comin'—RIP Michael K. Williams.

To all the women in this world who have had a scare, had or have cancer, had a bad gene test, whatever. To their families and friends, doctors, nurses, who cared for them: I send you a piece of my heart filled with love, encouragement, comfort, kindness, support, and thanks. Hell, you need a drink? I'll send you that too. I will send cookies, but not cocaine. Sorry boo!

And please know that no matter how much WE tie our boobs to our sense of self (let's skip society for now), they are not US. They don't tell the world anything about our hearts, souls, strengths, capabilities. Nothing.

Sure, they're pretty. But remember that what YOU are is beautiful regardless.

To MY people. You won't ever know the depth of my gratitude or how much I love you. I'm humbled, amazed, overwhelmed, and awed. All I can say is thank you. And if ever you need me, I'm right here. You have my whole heart, and you mean everything to me.

Your existence in this world keeps me sane and out of prison.

PS: No cancer for me this round. Let's hope it stays that way.

PPS: Eminem? Dang! Do you even need to ask? Love him. Greetings Mr. Mathers! But that's another conversation. I ramble y'all. I'm sure I didn't need to tell you.

Question: Who decided recipes needed to be novellas? And *when* was this decided? Recipes be like "I was walking through a wooded meadow as the sun was beginning its slow, evening descent. The fall colors were crisp and beautiful. The smell of autumn brought back the lush nostalgia of my childhood. This recipe will warm the cockles of your heart!" Umm, no the fuck it won't. But I do enjoy the word cockles.

About 8,000,000,000,000 adjectives later, there's an ad. On page 24 you get the recipe. For real? I do not give not one teeny tiny slip of a fuck about that meadow, Joanna, or any fucking cockles at this point. Just tell me how many fucking cups of sugar I need.

Am I a dick for this? You can tell me. But…

Don't

Don't tell me
I'm perfect or sublime
That my brilliance,
My charm, my élan
Renders you blind
That I'm so great
You can't take it
That your fate
Is bound forever
With mine
Keep your pedestal
High in the sky
Keep your absurdly
Honeyed words
I hold no desire
To be imprisoned
In such a place
A worded cage
Where I can't
Ever make a mistake
Where I'm forced
To mask my feelings
Hide my true face
Where my humanity
Isn't part of me
Like I'm some other
Thing
Separated from reality
No highs and lows
No ebb and flow
Not even a trace
Of anything off beam
A well of sameness
And placid insanity
With slick walls
Impossible to escape

I don't know how many times men, women too, but mostly men, have assumed what I would be like based on how I look. My music. What I would eat or drink. What I'd be into. What I wouldn't. How dumb is that?

They'd create this whole perfect version of me to fully subscribe to and build a reality around. Shockingly, they'd get supremely upset when I would do, say, wear, eat, think, or listen to something that didn't fit in the incorrect and idiotic little box they'd made for me. Unsubscribe.

Seriously had a guy come UNglued on me because he felt I was being untrue to my nature with the variety of music I enjoy. Another for using certain slang. And yet another because I am actually human and make mistakes. GTFOHRFNMF. (Get the fuck outta here, right fucking now, motherFUCKER.)

How dare I have flaws? How dare I be exactly who I am? Remember that I exist solely for me. But this bitch be trippin' I guess. Hewmans! Gross.

Dragon

I saw a black dragon in the clouds
With wings that stretched for miles
Gray smoke curled from his snout
There was blue fire in his eyes
His dark scales gleamed in the sky
His rider's head held high
Her arms thrown wide
She was so proud
How was she mounted?
I wondered if she
Had wings herself
I wanted desperately
To know their names
Surely, they had an earthly abode
They couldn't stay in the air forever
Could they?
Searching for a cave or stair
That might lead me to their lair
I drove and drove and drove
I climbed trees, and scaled mountains
I drank from a purple fountain
I ran until I lost my breath
I bribed and begged and lied
Day bled to night bled to day
On and on it went
Despair began to set
I knelt, broken at the edge
And there on my knees
She came to me!
I could barely raise my face
To look upon her was agony
A knowing of being less
Then her emerald gaze forgave
So at her unspoken command
I leapt!
Arms outflung
I briefly considered my demise
But when wings burst
From my very own back
I cried!
Excited to be unleashed
My wings took me high
Thin white clouds kissed *my* face
My fingertips brushed comets

I circled the yellow sun
Throughout the universe I raced
Exhilarated and lazy
All at once
Likely never to return

I was watching those birds I supposedly hate. Next thing I knew? This. Plus, I love dragons. I dream about them. Riding them. Rescuing them. They are majestic, friendly, elusive things in my dreams but lethal too. And a chick who rides dragons HAS to be a total badass.

I love to fly. In airplanes. I don't have wings. If I did, I would not be here with you peasants. I'm kidding. I would. A girl has to eat! I've heard there are some delicious peasant recipes on the Innanet. Or is it pheasant recipes? Hmm...

The universe enjoys poking at me. I've had some freaky, strange, weird, hilarious, sad, bizarre, joyful, get your thesaurus, encounters. I honestly think if someone told me this shit went down in their universe, I would be all "I'll take crazy bullshit that never happened for $1600, Alex." But I was there for all this and there are witnesses.

Tall Black Blonde

I didn't start drinking coffee until my thirties. Never had the taste for it. But going back to school again had me needing something. Anyway, I'm at Starbucks. No, I don't care if you hate Starbucks. Caribou was gone and there was nothing else close.

Barista: Welcome to Starbucks. What can I get started for you?
Me: I'll have a tall blonde holiday roast please.
Barista: Would you like room for cream?
Me: No thank you.
Barista: One tall, black, blonde please!
Me: Umm. That's me. I just ordered myself!

Half the line started cracking up. Some people looked scandalized. Really? Over that? Psssh.

Other dude behind the counter in a rush: OMG. I was thinking it but thought maybe it was racist. Don't be mad. You're so beautiful.

Me (brows raised):

His face was purple. I finally laughed and said it was cool. Toutes le monde ris! Got my coffee free. Laughed about it for days.

I share this because some people thought I should have been morally offended by the situation. Telling me how I should have gone off on the guy. Why? There was no malice. None. He got flustered. With all the racist encounters I've been through, I can tell the difference most of the time. Sometimes people just need a little grace. And by the way, how I respond to something is up to ME. Next!

Beige

Beige walls
Beige carpet
Beige couch
Family pictures strewn about
A decade worth of memories
Him, me, and the furry three
Staring out at the world
Looking so mother-fucking happy
There he sits
Glasses on his nose
So deeply engrossed
He rises to greet me
Smile on his handsome face
Tight squeeze
Kiss on the cheek
I look at him
Then it begins
Hey babe! Is that the latest Franzen you've got?
I agree, 'The Corrections' was great
Thanks for picking up dinner
But I'm not really hungry
Plus it's kinda late
No, I'd like a little chat
Tell me about your day
What did you do?
What did you say?
I know you love a conversation
Did you go anywhere?
Do something fun?
Did you have any errands to run?
The dishes still aren't done
I thought you were handling that
Hey, don't get all upset
It's just a question
But while we're at it
I have one more to ask
What the hell do you think you're doing?
Don't act dumb with me!
And don't tell me not to shout!
You know what I mean
Don't make this harder
Than it has to be
Working late, indeed!
I wasn't supposed to find out?

Did you just say that?
Out loud?
What is wrong with you?
And to cheat on me
With that thing?
Have you lost your fucking mind?
That bitch is more manly than you
Is that what you're into?
Let's see what else?
She's crass, and loud and rude
Not to mention ugly as fuck
Couldn't you have at least cheated up?
Maybe then I'd understand
Some hot, young thing
Caught your eye
The scotch was in the seat
You had some unmet need
But no! You!
You had to go and fuck
A loch ness cousin
How should I feel about that?
You do realize how many advances
I put a stop to?
For you?
Houses, boats, cash, jewelry
Declined! And why?
You love me?
You can explain?
Why should I believe
A single fucking word you say?
All I hear right now
Are lies and denial, but please
Explain to me
One time? I see!
Since it was just one time it's fine!
But you're still lying
I don't think you'd even
Know the truth if it hit you
Smack in the face
Like I want to
You needed 400 texts
For one night of sex?
All the constant messages?
Hey, married one!
Can you come out to play? She'd say
Such juvenile bullshit!
Your phone logs and emails
Are plenty of proof

Especially that
Hustler style picture
She sent to you
Did you bring her here?
Into my house?
Did you fuck her on our bed?
On your favorite beige couch?
Don't 'Honey, please' me!
You're *sorry*? It's not my fault?
Oh! Well what a relief!
It's not **my** fault my husband cheats!
Did you at least protect yourself?
You don't *think* you have anything?
I hope your dick falls off
Youprickdon'ttouchme!
I swear to God
You are such a piece of shit
I'd love to cut you
Cut all the lies right out
And her? Oh darling
I could kill her in her sleep
Or as I stared into her eyes
Wouldn't matter to me
Thirsting after married men
Should have some consequence
Don't you agree?
Perhaps a little kiss
The kind you like to give
Only with a Sig
I did leave her a lovely message
But she didn't reply
You look surprised
And a little scared
Why?
Did you think you could cheat?
Did you sneak that in the vows, somehow?
Change it to match your style?
It says forsaking all others,
Not fucking!
Well now I'm fucked *and* forsaken!
And isn't it just the best?
Funny
I never wanted this
These beige walls
This beige carpet

This fucking beige couch!
This life of a wife
But you walked in
Big green eyes
Big smile
Big…
Well, that was never our problem, was it?
You made me want it all
You made me believe
You made forever sound so feasible
I gave up everything for you
And what did I get?
This ring a twisted token
Promises turned to misery
Beige walls
Beige carpet

FUCKING BEIGE COUCH

I could almost laugh
If I wasn't so sad
As stupid as is it
I still love you
Even after all this
How could you even ask?
What good does it do?
I think you should go, now
I can't look at you
Because I think I hate you, too
And that's the worst of it
Go where? WHERE!

I Don't Fucking Care!
Go be with that thing
Go sleep on the street
Just get out PLEASE!
Just leave

Every single day
I rehearse this confrontation
In the shower, in my car, in my brain
I rehearse it
A thousand different ways
I'm so ready!
To end this
And go on my way
But the words
Are stuck in my mouth

And I can't seem
To force them out
This is not what I wanted
But it's what I have
Beige walls
Beige carpet
Fucking beige couch

I couldn't bear to put all of the stuff with this on paper.

My pen refused too, because I think he knew I didn't want to dig back into those days after I'd so narrowly escaped them.

I may have been experiencing a moment of pique when I wrote this. Or maybe a moment of angry pity. You run the gamut of useless and destructive emotions.

Feeling ugly, unwanted, insecure, rejected. Foolish. Asking yourself asinine questions. What a nasty and toxic ball of absolute shit.

If you haven't heard, the cheating likely has zero to do with you. It doesn't matter how rich, beautiful, handsome, kind, loving, smart, or talented you are. It doesn't matter how much he gets his duck sick or how many bracelets you buy her.

In my case, fences are mended now. I didn't want to go to jail and it's just not worth it.

And yeah, I turned down cars, houses, vacations, you name it, from other men. Those things mean less than nothing if the rest isn't there.

Cheaters? Never mind. You won't listen anyway. Just go to hell with gasoline draws on. Do not pass go. Collect a kick in the ass. In the throat too.

Question: When did casual cruelty become commonplace? When did acting like a complete jackass in public become cool? That is two questions. I see people behaving like there are no consequences. Out there acting like they ain't got a lick of gotdamn sense. What is happening?

Instead of shunning these people, we glorify them. Make memes and videos. Then these assholes make money. For being assholes. FRD? What planet am I on?

And why is everyone always so ready to cut another person down? This goes back to my miserable fucks comment, I guess.

Seems to me that people are perched at home like deranged keyboard vultures waiting to attack or hoping for someone to make a little mistake so they can properly berate them as loudly as possible. Or shit, for someone to be doing nothing at all so they can insert themselves and create drama where none existed. Do people get off on this hateful ass, petty, ridiculous, shit? I have angry moments, we all do, but this is way out of hand.

This is for sure a FAFO scenario with me. Do not. The result will be drastic. I will make you hate your own skin, then write a nasty poem about you.

Dangerous Angel

The green scrawl
On the bathroom wall
Screams at me
"Love Is A Dangerous Angel!"
So I took a moment
To ponder what the intent
Of such a statement
Could be
But then
In a purple pen
The words
"We've become"
Grabbed my attention
Well, I found myself
Pondering once again
Become what?
I only became
Filled with discontent
As I could not
Figure
What was meant
My dissatisfaction grew
Because next to that
In glaring blue
Big as it could be
Was "Let me love you"
Stunned as I was to see
Invitation so plainly
To something
So blatantly false
It didn't stop me
From reading
"Jackie" had been there
And recently
From what I could tell
Someone else
Referenced Poe
And his brazen bells
Fascinated and titillated
Nonplussed by the time
I journeyed, quietly
Into other people's minds
Sara's heartbreak unmade me
I nearly cried

But like a child
I was soon distracted
By the next attraction
Just then
There was a knock
"Are you ok in there,
It's been a while?"
Annoyed
I grabbed my pink lipstick
As I had nothing else
To write with
Quickly, I scribbled
A delicious, philosophical inscription
Leaving no explanation
For the next pedestrian
Who graces this station
And falls victim
To the scrawl
On the bathroom wall

Barnes & Noble. Spent too long out. Had to pee. I hate peeing in public. Hey, I don't care where you go or how clean the restroom seems. Someone that ain't me sat on that bowl. Anyway, I went in, got one of those butt paper for your toilet seat thingies and sat down. There was all this writing on the door and the wall. Most of it was your basic unintelligible trash, but I saw dangerous angel in big green letters. There you go.

PS: I didn't have any lipstick and I surely didn't write on the wall.

Dating Is a Bitch

After our conversation
Exchange of information
I find I'm perplexed
On what to do next
Do I send a text?
Is an email best?
Is that long gone?
Do folks still use a phone?
Do I send incessant salvos?
Just so you know
I think you're swell
Hell, do people still say swell?
Should I wait?
Not call too soon
I don't want a stalker tag
Or you to think I'm a creep
All this uncertainty
Is bound to be
The end of you and me
Before we begin
Despite all this messiness
I take the fall, make a call
We have another chat
Before you know it
Our date is set
Dinner and drinks
Sound good, I think
Pick you up in my truck
Watch as your long legs
Swing onto the seat
We talk more
You blush a lot on the ride
What's that about?
Are you being coy with me?
Over dinner
Our hands absently touch
There's that blush
I think I like
What I see in your eyes
Then suddenly it's over
Dinner's been eaten
Drinks are drunk
It was all so fast
I drive you home

Walk you to your door
But here again
I'm unsure
Do we shake hands, hug?
Share a kiss? Cheek or lips?
Should I call you again?
What is the rule on this?
Mike P. had it right
Indecision clouds my vision
And though I had a very nice
Time with you tonight
I'm utterly convinced
That dating is a bitch

Dating is stupid and brutal. I don't envy you guys. Some of you I want to punch in the esophagus, repeatedly, but I don't envy any of you. There are so many unspoken rules that change by the minute, by the woman. And for us, the dating game is more of a war. Lots of little battles. Whole Bunch of Fuckery.

Mike Patton's voice makes me happy. Damn!

Charcoal

The scene: Yet another expensive restaurant in downtown Cincinnati. My date is a doctor. Tall, handsome. I have to say, yours truly looks damn expensive too. I'm so cute. I'd go out with me in a blink. He grabs my hand and twirls me around to look at me on arrival. Yeah, he did. Strike one.

Anyway. We're seated.

The waiter comes immediately. Kind. Funny. Professional. Gives the specials, goes over the wine list. Dude is out of the gate rude and nasty to the waiter. I hate that. Who do you think you are? Strike two.

Him: We'll have the Cabernet.
Waiter: Yessir.
Me: I'd like some water please, no Cabernet.
Him: She'll have the Cabernet.
Me: SHE will not have Cabernet. SHE has allergies.

I'm smiling but it's that strained psychotic version you see in movies before somebody get they thote cut. I'm a tad annoyed, but whatevs. I'm trying to keep strike three at bay.

Him: Oh, I see.
Waiter leaves.
Him: You look lovely.

I don't even get the thank you out before dude embarks on a journey of verbal and unmitigated self-love. According to him, he's AMAZING! A real catch. Well-off. Well-endowed. Yeah, he hinted at it. I'm bored. I want to drop *him* in a well. I'm trying to be cool though. The waiter comes back and this foo (it's supposed to be foo) tries to order my appetizer and my dinner! Nah homie. I explain that I appreciate the effort, but he doesn't know me well enough for that. I'm super annoyed. I order the most expensive items I see. The waiter leaves again and guess what this donkey says? GUESS!

Him: See, I do not date black women. But you are an exception. You have beautiful light skin, you are intelligent, and not loud like them.
Strike 4,495,763
Me: 'Scuse me? Fuck did you just say?
I'm basically hissing, and I know my face is all kinds of fucked up. You could have shoved a plate in each nostril.
Him: What's the problem? That's a compliment. You should—
Me: You stupid, lowbrow, classless, fuckfaced, ridiculous, asshole. *You* don't date black women? You look like burnt charcoal. Goodbye.
I tend to string insults together when I'm furious. I stood up and he told me to sit down.

OH NO HE MUTHAFUCKIN' DIDN'T!

Young me would have thrown my water or slapped his face. Calmer me found the waiter. Told him what was up. I doubled my order of: Lobster—market price, filet mignon, side salad with grilled shrimp. Dessert. Everything ala carte. Hell, a spoonful of mashed potatoes was $15. I told the waiter to take it home. I left and got a cheeseburger.

I've had men tell me to my face that they don't date white women, black women, tall women, pick my attribute, while they're on a date with **me**. Followed by some bullshit like, but you're so pretty, so well spoken, so intelligent. Like I'm supposed to feel special now because they've chosen me despite their petty little prejudices. GTFOHMF.

Saying shit like that is the fastest way to make hate you. Look out for the stranger on the train.

And yes, you can have preferences but why even ask *me* out if you have them? **STEWPID!**

Homie got his PhD at BAU. That's Bitch Ass University for y'all who are wondering.

Swing

Blue, cloudless sky
Skirt hiked up high
Long legs dangle
A peek of thigh
Maybe even a sneak
Of cotton or lace
Blush on her face
As she swings
Her laughter rings
And the sun rays play
On her golden frame
He is lost to the world
No desire to go back
Only needing her
At this moment
She is everything
His heart, his joy
His eternity
Young and impossibly free
She is his dream
In the flesh

When I was little, my big sister would take me to Eden Park to swing. She would always get me a treat. It was our time together. I pull up those memories when I'm struggling. And yeah, I enjoy going to the park even though I'm allergic to every damn thing there.

One day I was walking in the park and saw an older couple near the swing set. To my complete joy, the woman got on. The man with her watched her swing and so did I. He loved her and I could see it. I couldn't help myself. I wandered over and talked to them.

Married for a billion years, 3 grown children, bunch of grandkids. They'd had their trials like anyone else, but you could tell it made them stronger together. I hugged them. I told them I thought they were wonderful. How nice it was to see love like theirs in real life. I wanted to spend the day with them. They were so beautiful to me. I wanted to scream and cry.

I Love You

If I begin
By saying I love you
Do the words that follow
Sparkle
Like wet grass in the sun?
If I finish with I love you
Do the prior words
Linger
Like a song on your heart?
Is I love you the key
That opens every door
Or does it simply allow the possibility?
Is it a lock
Keeping you chained to me?
Is I love you
The beginning or the end?
Can it work for everything between?
Does saying I love you
Let me behave like a snake?
Can I treat you like a god
Yet withhold the words you crave?
Does I love you
Fill the holes in your soul?
Or make a dent in your wall?
I'm confused and don't know truly
How these words feel to *you*
Still, for good or ill
From toes to face
However you choose
To interpret the news
I love you

People put such a strange emphasis on I love you. I've seen people throw it out as casually as hello while others nearly implode over the mere thought of saying it. Some use it like a weapon.

You never know how someone will receive it. The spiral can go in any direction. It's such a weighty thing.

Relationships rise and fall over these words. There's songs and books and a whole industry built up on I love you.

FYI: Nothing makes me more homicidal (is that possible?) than someone who falsely uses I love you to manipulate me. It's repulsive and unnecessary. But, if you tire of your existence and desire to shed your mortal coil early, gone head, FAFO.

Absolution

Fully divested
I rested
At the edge
Of my bed
Waiting, bated
Contemplating
Wanting to end
This season
of treason
Not knowing how
Wanting to bend
My mind
around the reasons
of where I am now
Needing to see
A future
that included
Some solution,
A kind of
resolution
But if it came
Would I know
my absolution?
Would I leave this place?
Abandon the anger
Release the hate
Spit out
the bitter pill
that swallowed me
hollowed me
Clear the ichor
from my veins?
Say goodbye
to the prison
in my mind
Or will I remain
Tethered
On this hellish plane
like a dog
On a choking chain
Snapping, snarling, hurling
Using all my might
Barking fruitlessly
Into the night

The moon shining high
Gives no insight
No direction
Just her reflection
Sterile and cold
Like my naked flesh
Unmoved
and unmoving
As if I need
Some unseen thing
To rouse the fire
Seething deep
Beneath this cheerless casing
Erase and eradicate
This shroud so utterly
Revealing me
As I used to be

Tragedy and betrayal change us. The mirror shows someone you barely know. It's your face but it's not you. The eyes are darker, the smile is a lie. You wonder how to get that 'other' person back. That person who would smile and laugh. That person with intelligent conversation and joyful eyes. You. Before tragedy, before betrayal. You. Before.

Unfortunately, some of us get stuck there. Used to, and almost enjoying, the bleakness of it. Self-martyrdom. It's easier than working to get free.

But I did the work. I love myself. I love my life. The past is merely a lesson. I own the future.

Killer

A pretty little bird
Saved my life because she
Ate up the killer bee
Heading straight for me
Snatched it right out of the sky
Gobbled it all up
Without a blink
Sat down, fluffed and strutted
It was freaking sweet
It filled me with glee
Killer bee! Psssh! Please!
I know it seems
Hard to believe
She was looking out
For this curly haired lout
And not her own
Little bird belly, but
I swear, as she again
Took wing to air
She winked
Over top her little bird beak

All I can say is that I'm with you now because of that bird. She took care of my light work. I put this in here because I was actually scared of that stupid insect. I was mad at myself later but realized that was silly so I wrote this for my savior bird.

Question: Ever meet your favorite singer, actor, writer, whatever and they were a complete dick? Did you continue to like/support them afterward?

Me? I've had the occasion to meet a host of famous folks. By accident, at work, just out and about, and of course on purpose. Met this writer at a book signing. He's dead so I won't say his name. But! What a condescending, arrogant, self-righteous, preachy, out of touch, weird as fuck, annoying twatwaffle. I left without getting my book signed. Lame.

Thought about it. Figured maybe he just had a bad day. Caught the tour in another city I happened to be in. Same shit. Never bought or read another book.

On the flip, I've met R. A Salvatore and Barry Eisler. Both were kind, funny, down to earth, and engaging. No ego, no attitude. Genuinely nice. I was 'mad' at R. A. for killing off a character, but he got me over it by being so wonderful. Hats off to you two for being awesome. I still buy/read/promote your books. Both of you are better writers than dead dude.

You guys remember I ramble right? There's a point here. I can't imagine how hard it is to be famous. People always wanting a picture, an autograph, to talk to you, touch you. No space. No peace. Everyone is not cut out for that life.

I had a micro taste of it. Freaked Me Out. It's the clichéd double-edged sword. You're famous because folks love (obsess over) what you do. If they didn't, you wouldn't be famous.

Here's the thing. We all need to remember that our favorite celebs are people too. They have good days and bad.

They might like five minutes to themselves to eat without having to smile for you or sign your t-shirt. They might need a break from the constant prying and judgment. Imagine how you would feel if every time you left the house, you were mobbed by strangers. If every action was publicly judged.

I saw Snoop at the Las Vegas airport once. You think I didn't want to run up to him? Of course I wanted to. I love him. But I just smiled/nodded at him and went on my way.

PS: If you ever meet me and *I'm* being a dick, I've either had an absolute shit day and can't fake it or you're being a dick too. Sumaya'll shouldn't interact with other hewmans.

PPS: Dick goes for dudes and chicks. It's not anatomy.

At Rest

Each day I watch
A thousand hats
Fall upon his head
He takes them all
Doesn't break a sweat
He's strong and smart
Honest and sweet
He's always everything
Everyone
Needs him to be
No complaints
Pass his lips
Just does what he does
Flawlessly
But right now
He's lying here
So peacefully
Next to me
Soulful eyes shut tight
Against the light
From a lamp outside
A crooked half smile
Tilts his handsome face
He's in a peaceful place
Dreams have taken him
Where this life cannot
The stresses of his day
Have faded away
Frowns don't crease his brow
The world's woes
Don't trouble him now
His powerful shoulders
Carry nothing heavier
Than the old tee
He sleeps in
The broad chest
Simply rises and falls
With each breath
I take pleasure
In seeing him like this
This beautiful man
Finally at rest

Screenshots

Back to that dating thing. These are bad text conversations on my dummy phone. I'm not a total idiot, none of these foos got a date. I mostly responded for the comedy.

Him: Hello gorgeous
Me: Hello
Him: Did you play any sports?
Me: I used to
Him: I love the way you look. I bet you have strong legs.
Me: I guess so
Him: I bet you can't kick me in the dick and make me cry
Me thinking it's a joke: I'm more of a caregiver so the world will never know
Him: Seriously. I bet you can't do it. If you really hurt me, I'll pay you.
Me: Go away. I'm not interested.
Him: You're scared. I'll come to you.
Me: If you had any sense, YOU would be the one scared. Fuck off, dude.

Okay penis owners? Is this a thing? Why would you WANT to get kicked in the dick? I can't imagine any scenario where this makes sense. I'm concerned about sumay'all. Deeply.

And I hate when dudes I don't know are like Hey beautiful. Hey gorgeous. Blech. Use my name until you know me better. Honest compliments are always okay, but y'all get ridiculous with this.

Him: I herd that
Me: You work on a farm?
Him: LOLOLOLOL no. Why you say that for?
Me: Never mind, son

I don't have to explain this, do I?

Him: I have a 9' tongue and can breath threw my ears
Me: This isn't an interview for the circus
Him: I joss wanna plesure you if you let me
Me: What does plesure mean?
Him: You know, make you feel good
Me: I'd feel fantastic if you could spell

His tongue is 9' huh? Wonder where he puts it during the day? Breath threw? FRD

Him: I am your knight in shiny armor
Me: Shining
Him: Huh?
Me: Shining, not shiny

Him: I don't get it

Me: No, you don't.

I love that meme "I wanted a knight in shining armor but ended up with an asshole in tinfoil."

Do you guys really have no idea how to talk to women? Does any of this shit work, EVER?

I wish I had taken pictures of my face when I was reading some of this trash.

Zero

At a bar in downtown Cincinnati
The guy is hot. We already know I am (wink!). I have a cherry coke; he has a whiskey. We'd been talking about paint drying in winter for thousands of minutes. I'm disappointed because dude is a *lot less* intelligent in person and his conversation skills are abysmal. I'm wondering if someone else was talking to me online. *And* he keeps licking his lips. Nasty.

Him: How many dates we have to go on before we fuck?
He's leaned over and leering.
Me (smiling): Zero, because if I had a bottle, I would break it on this bar and stab it into your face.

Umm. I still don't know why I said face. I was thinking neck.

Him:
Me: Have a great evening, Zero

Admittedly, I was the tiniest bit pissy that night. I didn't want to go to a bar, it was hot and humid, my hair was hateful.
But I'd also had a guy show up 30 years older, a dick pic sharer, a Mr. Handsy I had to threaten, one who showed up dirty, and yet another who tried to 50 Shades me. Within two weeks. Fucking hell. The 50 Shades story is hilarious! Cringily saying Vol II.

Thanks-Giving!

Presented
With this food Wonderland
I feel a lot like Alice
Though without the Queen
And all her malice
The table's piled high
Turkey and ham and yams
My goodness!
It smells so heavenly
Before I can take my seat
The provisions shriek
Clamoring
Eat ME!
Drink ME!
I swear that pie
Is staring into my eyes
Trying to hypnotize
And how could I
A mere mortal, deny
Hey wait!
Did a rabbit just go by?
You didn't see it?
Never mind
With no volition
My limbs extend
Gather up
Pieces of the feast
Scrumptious rump of roast beast
I have no choice
I must partake
Past my lips it goes
When oh no
I feel my waist
Expanding
I'm glad I'm wearing
These stretchy pants
Damn!
I need to back away
But I waited
No, I trained
For this very day
To totally stuff my face!
But I must also
Give thanks

To the Heavens above
To the people I love
You make my life so bright
And because I have you…
Hey, these calories don't count
Right?

Most holidays, I write something. I'm usually in a good mood and I can be unbelievably silly.

Don't ask what sent me spiraling off to Alice in Wonderland. It's funny how the mind works. Especially the one under all these curlies.

Holi-Daze

The Christmas holiday
Has been so hazy
Because I
Have been so lazy!
Shopping
At the 11th hour
With all the crazies
Flipping off
Strangers over
Parking spaces
Elbows rubbed
The wrong way at Macy's
Insults imagined at Dicks
Is that a Freudian slip?
Funny me
Wait till you see what's next!
Oh yeah, the loft?
It's a mess, I declare
Bags, bows, and toile
All over the place
Miles of tape everywhere
But hey I decorated
My stripper pole!
Priorities are my thing
But despite all this
Busy-ness
I spent some time
In my kitchen
Cookies, pies, cakes, candy
You name it!
All made from scratch
Come get some if you can
And when you stop by
Please don't forget
A few long hugs
And maybe a kiss
I'm giving out lots of love
That's the real reason
For this season
Forget shopping and
Mall hopping madness
Leave your worry at my door
Relax a moment, be cared for
That is my wish for you

And a Merry Christmas!

I LOVE CHRISTMAS!

Each year I bake for 3 or 4 days. My home is open. I love having visitors. This was a public announcement of that, and me poking a little fun at the insanity. This particular year I lived in a loft with a giant pole through the middle.

I hate holiday shopping. Hewmans are mean, rude, cruel, hateful things when it should be a time for kindness and care. And why? Deals on useless shit? Brilliant!

Reese's

There's this bag
Of Reese's eggs
Between my legs
Probably getting hot
From my, uh, never mind
I have no shot of not
Eating the whole fucking thing
The Reese's peeps
Have it in for me
They think I need
The diabeetus
Or acne at 43
Whoever Will is
He's left the building
With his power
Laughing
I know I've lost
When my eighth egg
Of the hour
Disappears
Into oblivion

Don't you judge me. Those things are evil. And they jump out of the bag naked. Sneaky little bastards.

Dead to Me

Secrets kept unsafely
Lips loosened in haste
A sunken friendship
You gave me away
For five seconds of fame
There is no apology
You've said plenty
Go off and play
In a bottomless grave
You are dead to me

"A source close to." GTFOH. Lemme tell you right now, there is no source closer to me than me. Anyone talking to you about me? Probably doesn't know jack.

If someone's got some juicy gossip, they might have some Clorox infused dog shit oil to pour down your throat, too. But you're an adult so you go ahead and swallow whatever you like.

How 'bout this, though? If you're close to someone, why would you ever want to hurt them? Are you that loathsome of a carbon form? That a dollar means more to you than a person you're supposedly close to? Or are you just drawn to the attention it brings? A whole ten seconds of relevance. At what expense? SMMFH.

The reasons do NOT matter. Because either way, that's another of those FAFO scenarios with me. I'm not interested in sorry. Shove that sorry in your hole.

Come In

My what a surprise
To be seeing you again
Sure, come on in
Be welcome
Take off your hat
Leave your coat
On the peg by the door
Slip off your shoes
Like you used to
Please have a seat
Can I get you a drink?
Perhaps a bite to eat?
You don't want anything?
Only to talk?
Oh, I see
Well, I'll listen, but
I tell you this is strange
It's been so long
Since I saw your face
The last I knew
You were leaving
Going to find your meaning
Find your place
Nothing would bring you back
That was a year ago
If it was a day
Pray tell me what it is
That's brought you all this way
Before you begin
Let me say
My tears went dry
The second you said goodbye
My heart didn't break
As I sat here in the darkness
I didn't have to fake happiness
I had it in spades
I didn't waste my nights
Dreaming you were by my side
I couldn't have cared
That you weren't there
I haven't waited
I've moved on, I've grown,
I've never been alone
No, no, no

Do not hold me
That's not your right
Don't kiss me that way
Don't melt away my objections
Don' t let me hear your heartbeat
Or feel the warmth of your skin
But most importantly
Don't say you love me
Because if you do
I might admit
That I still love you

Break-ups are hard. Saying hello after saying goodbye can be equally devastating. There's familiarity mixed with uncertainty. When someone hurts you, you know, whether you admit it or not, they could do it again and easily. Old memories cloud judgment. For me, though? Once I say goodbye, that's the end. I don't and I won't play that game. This is simply my imagining of what it might be like to bend.

Toxic thing about me and break-ups? I pre-break-up. When I figure out I'm done, I start getting blah and weird. I check out mentally. I mourn the relationship and start moving on emotionally. I'm less caring about the small details (what you like on your sandwich type shit). I say things I normally wouldn't. I'm not the same woman you met. Basically, I quit being myself. It's total asshole behavior. We can get into that later.

I wonder sometimes if there's something wrong with me. I easily cut people off and move on. I don't think of them again or care what happens to them either. I can't be the only one. Definitely a trauma response, but is it too much?

A Friend Request

1 new friend request
Yup, that's what
The message said
And it seemed to be
Kind and benign
At the time
You liked a photo that's cool
Sent a private message
On Sunday, okay!
Then a week later, it changed
You got deranged
Started acting strange
Crazy talking, cyber stalking
You were in love
It was fate
I was destined
To be your mate
Did I love you too?
Fuck and **NO**, though
Isn't there a song or two
About this kind of thing
Bugaboos and spider webs
Driving folks to extremes
Why'd you have to be that way?
You could have just behaved
Instead of showing your ass
Your utter lack of class
No decorum in the forum
Did you display
Perturbing and disturbing me
Every single day
I tried the nice route
That didn't work out
You trampled on my kindness
Acted like a mindless beast
No choices left
Time to unfriend, unsubscribe
Banish, make you vanish
A click here
A click there
Erase you from everywhere

Block, delete, undo, remove
Anything I can do
To get rid of you
Forever

This is the direct result of my own personal Facebook stalker. Don't be jealous. Before I learned how to block everything, this little loony bird decided she was in love with me, and I was in love with her. The pictures were FOUL. No, I mean it. I still get the heebs when I think about it. Heebs!

My Friend, My Brother

Lately I've been having dreams
Revisiting the memories
Of the you that used to be
My friend, my brother
Riding our big wheels
Down a hill too steep
Risking fatal injury
Just to feel the summer breeze
Transformers and Star Wars
No Barbie, no sir
Didn't we bury her under the fort?
Laughing, hiding, trying to fly
Tadpoles, bugs, random stuff
Smushed in sopping pockets
Driving mama bear nuts
The trouble we got into!
But I had you
You had me
That was all I needed
Fall flew by in a blink
School and associated things
The days grew long and dark
Soon it was Winter
Some new friends came
You became a stranger
Anger, sadness, and betrayal
Replaced love and trust
Bonds forged by blood were broken
I longed for the you I knew
And those friends
They're not the heroines of the story
Just evil things, soulless, uncaring
They left you buried
Deep in the snow
But I'm the one who's cold
And I will never again know
The you that used to be
But I dream
And I remember

My youngest brother was bipolar schizophrenic. Being a black man in those days was hard enough, still is.

Add mental illness, self-medication, and shady 'friends'. You can fucking forget anything resembling a happy ending.

I didn't understand schizophrenia when I was a kid. As an adult, so much damage had been done that I had difficulty letting go of my anger and feelings of betrayal. The horrendous fights and terrible stretches of silence. A part of my spirit shriveled and went dark.

Now he's gone. Some days I hate him for leaving me.

Other days I thank him.

I don't talk about it much. The pain knocks me down sideways and I can't think or breathe. It's never hits when I expect it. Why would it?

About a year after he died, I saw a man who looked like him. I had to go to my car and cry. It took me over an hour to get it back together. I'm not really a crier, but that day I put lie to that. Fuck.

In Love

His chest
Hard beneath my fingers
His lips
Soft against my tongue
Our hips touch
And we laugh
We're just lying here
Completely in love
With one another

Remember when I talked about wishful thinking? Here we go again. Not to say I haven't experienced love. The visual this puts into my head is like those soft, gauzy romance scenes in the movies. I've never done THAT. I need to. For research purposes.

Threnody

Threnody
A creation sought
To bring release
Of hurt etched deep
Hanging heavily
In the air
Melancholy
Full of despair
And yet
Impossibly sweet
Love and pain
Inextricably linked

I was waiting for a funeral procession to go by. I saw a woman in a car. Her windows were down. She was crying, laughing, and singing. She was lovely to me. It teared me up. I sent well wishes into the universe for her.

As unpopular as it will make me, I am never going to another funeral. I don't understand them and never will. I find the funeral business predatory. $4k for a silk pillow? FUCK YOU funeral home. I will go to a life celebration, a party, a whatever. I will come sit next to you for hours after it's over, but no more funerals for this curly girl.

Question: Ever wondered if you've suddenly started speaking in a lost Mesopotamian language? How many times have you heard yourself utter "That's not what I'm asking, that's not what I said, that's not what I mean."

Don't worry. You're still speaking English or whatever your native language is. The problem is that People Don't Fucking Listen. They've got their fingers jammed into their noses, their asses, their phones. They're off in their own little land where ears are used for cooking or some shit. You can watch as they get all poised to answer the question they *think* you're going to ask. But you didn't fucking ask THAT and now YOU have to EXPLAIN. Or they seize one irrelevant thing they kinda heard and start going off in a different direction. Even better is when they start answering before you get there. It's infuriating and insane.

It leads to misinformation, distrust, and drama. That he said/she said shit goes pear-shaped real quick. STEWPID.

How hard is it to fucking listen? I've decided to stop talking to people who consistently fail in that regard. It's too much work with zero reward.

I would like to spend a day listening. To Neil deGrasse Tyson talk to me about the cosmos; to Neil Gaiman read me a book; to a 90-year-old man or woman tell me about their life; to my friend tell me about their day; to my mother, my sister, my brother tell me anything; to a 5 year old tell me about cartoons; to a veteran tell me something that brought him or her joy in a dark time.

I want to fill myself with the experiences and wisdom of others. Then I want to do it again with a new group on new topics.

FYI: I named my iPad Neil. Every iPad will be named Neil.

Gram-er?

Truly bad grammar makes me crazy(er). We all screw up, but geez! Seeing should of, could of, would of? Agony! I'm an independent women! You mean you and all your personalities? I seen it! Did you? Because I saw it. It's between him and I. Nope. It Is Not. There's so many. Let's not even talk about they're, their, there, then, than, and irregardless.

Wait! Fellas! Which girl do you want? I'd rather cuddle than have sex, or I'd rather cuddle then have sex. It's an important distinction.

But I wrote these and laughed like an idiot the whole time. An idiot!

Last Knight

Last knight eye dee sided two Taiwan awn
Witch turned inn too a miss steak
Sew much whine and nut thing two eat
Does knot a happy mourning make
Lettuce just say that my head is pounding,
Lick her has lost it's a peel
Plus eye cant fined the tile and all!
Eye knead two git my mined rite
Yet eye cant seam too faux cuss
I'm going inn Seine width the pane
May bee eye should think bee four eye drink

Kit Tee

Yesterday my kit tee had an axe a dent
He roled down the stares and baroque his foot
Bye the thyme we maid it two the vet
My pour kit tee was inn ex stream ago knee
Sitting inn emergence sea is sew nerve-wracking
What a knight mare!
Butt the dock was the vary sole of patients
She banned edged his foot and cent us home width a warning
"Bee mined full on the stares width your pause!"
If he had dent bin sew hurt, it wood of bin hill larry us

Spell check is pissed at me even now.

Surcease

In his arms
I find peace
Surcease
Of all that ails me
The ills of this world
Cannot assail me
The darkness that attempts
Is forced to fade
As I lie here, content

Have you ever had someone really hold you? Until all the stress, tension, anger, and sadness just slid out of your body?

My mom and sister used to lie me across their laps and beat this rhythm on my back when I was little. It remains one of the most calming things I've ever felt.

Burn

Kisses burn
I fall
Hearts pulse
I wait
Questions
Become reasons
Memory strings
Lure me
To things forgotten
A lover's touch
A smile's taste
I give pause
I wonder how
I've come
To this illicit place
Where time drips away
In reverse
I pray for an end
I long for release

How many times can I use I got nothin' before you get truly annoyed? I really don't know here. Could have been a 4 AM brain fizzle. Could have been me thinking this was epic. Don't know folks. Big curly shrug.

Winter

Winter sings to me
Cold kisses on my lips
His ice fills my mouth
As snowflakes fall
I raise arms and eyes to him
A child again, beseeching
Winter barks a dark laugh
Seeing me in supplication
He knows he can take me
To his windswept cave
He knows I couldn't escape
That I would succumb
To his frozen embrace
But today
His fingers simply stroke my face
Reminding me that I can play
But I must obey, be wary
As he is danger
I wonder why I love him

Went skiing once. Almost got frostbite. Vowed to never go again. I hate being cold but oddly I love winter landscapes. The stark beauty. Desolate and dangerous, but so lovely. Snowcapped mountains? A field covered in snow? Makes me feel serene. If you ask me to go out in said field, you might get stabbed. Or, I might run out there and make snow angels. You have to decide if you'll accept either fate. Honestly though, I'm forever that bitch chillin' in the cabin with cocoa. Winter will not be catching me out like that!

But this isn't about that either. Sorry folks.

Unmade

Paying for mistakes
I didn't make
Giving all I am
Not to forsake
The vow of love I made
Destruction comes
In the form of words
Thrown like acid
On a stone
You see no damage
Until it breaks
And it's entirely too late

Me and my dating mistakes! So, here's my dumbass again dating a guy I shouldn't be. He would get mad about nothing and start an argument. He was a petty little bitch. He would say the most venom-laced, nasty shit. Name-calling (everyone was stupid but him), throwing every dagger, hateful as all hell. One day, mid-rant, I said, "Ok. Bye." He was so confused. Where was I going? Why was I leaving? I laughed and told him to never call me again. He didn't listen. Couldn't believe I'd let him go over a few stupid words, him being so great. Boy, fuck you still.

I don't understand people who go at others with the intention to hurt and destroy, then want to take it back once they feel better. Nope. Once is all you get with me. Y'all need to get your prepositions sorted. Come to me? We good. You can say almost anything to me if you say it right. Come at me? Congratulations. You just unlocked a level of hell that even Dante was not familiar with.

Trust that you will not enjoy the experience.

I don't say things I don't mean. Not. Ever. If I told you I only want the best for you always, that every single day be filled with love and happiness, I meant it. If I told you I wanted you to die painfully and alone, gasping, not found for days, with your thirteen cats pissing on your rotting corpse, I meant it. No matter how sweet or how harsh. I. Meant. It.

Get Off

"Oh yeah, baby. Oh God, you're so good. Oh wow. Yeah, yeah."

How did I end up here, with this stupid pig grunting on top of me? Slobbery kisses down the side of my face. Clumsy awkward hands fumbling my bits. The adolescent chatter.

The inadequate parts. Where did I find this moron and why the fuck did I bring him home?

I'm being unfair. There isn't anything wrong with him. Or his parts, I guess. I'm hungry. I haven't eaten in days. It's made me vicious.

Getoffgetoffgetoffgetoffgetoffgetoffgetoff

"Huh? What are you saying," he asks.
"I said get off."
"What, come right now?"
"No idiot. Get the fuck off me."
"Aww, don't be like—"
"Get off and get out."
Rick? Or is it Joe? Is shocked. I can feel the confusion. He has no idea what's going on. He thought he was going to have a good night. Sorry, Rick. Or Joe. Whoever. As he's reaching for his clothes, I feel the shift. Hurt now. Maybe angry. Mumbling. Calling me every kind of bitch. No problem, I can definitely take him if he gets out of hand.
"Hey buddy? Don't leave any of your shit behind, k?"
"What is your problem, lady?"
"Jesus, are you still here?"
"Well, fuck you, then!"
"You failed there. Do you at least know how to cook?"
My cruelty saved that man's life. If he had stayed here, I wouldn't have been able to stop myself from eating him, clothes and all. It's what I am. I don't know how to be anything else. I have not yet become fully human. And people saw me with him. They can't find me. I have to stay safe until the transition.

Go

I didn't come
So you have to go
Coffee
Is for closers

The little story is something I might expand on one day. But remember, I have squirrel brain. Get Off—subtle ode to Prince.

Shortest poem ever about, well, you know. I imagine the chick, or dude, who would say this to someone, and I am in love. Unless they said it to me. Then, I don't know. I could laugh hysterically or beat them with my shoe. Crap shoot!

Chair

Exhaustion sits on me
Its limbs splayed
Butt firmly planted
No remedy
No relief
Just pressing
I set a breaking pace
In what wasn't
Even a race
Now I am a chair
A stupid fucking chair
A seat for exhaustion
Who doesn't even care

This is the direct result of being mentally, emotionally, and physically tired. Why was I being that ridiculous? My body and brain were screaming at me to rest. I didn't. Made a whole bunch of fucked up mistakes.

Well, that's what I get. Maybe you'll see what kind of stupidity I got into with Vol II.

Steps

Sweat
Soaks my simple cotton dress
As I climb concrete steps
Warm air blows my curly hair
Licks at my face
I turn and see the city
Spread out beneath me
People going about, doing things
Unaware that I'm watching
Lights in windows
Shadows on the street
A little dog crosses my path
Bark, bark, bark!
He's broken my reverie
I pet his furry head and he's off
He's made me laugh
I share his excitement, only
My legs are tired
I think of turning around, giving up
The steps didn't seem many
But my dress grows heavy
It's suffocatingly hot
The humidity stifles me
And the sweat
Now drips so that
If I were to rest
It would pool beneath my feet
Then I hear the church bell ring
Challenging me
To finish the steps
To continue climbing
To reach
To let my sweat
Be absorbed
Into these steps of history
These steps
Where I can turn and see
Cincinnati
Spread out beneath me

Even though I don't live in Cincinnati anymore, it will always be my home. The view from the top of these steps in Mt. Adams is stunning. For whatever reason, I decided to climb those steps in a dress. In the heat. And humidity. My hair was fucked up y'all! But! It inspired this so no harm. Except maybe to the folks who caught a whiff of me on the way down. Small farm animal-ish aroma. Blech!

If you ever go to my hometown, get some Graeter's and Aglamesis Bros. Go to Eden Park. Look at the beautiful Italianate architecture. EAT! The food is amazing. The skyline is my favorite. There is plenty to see and do.

Then go home. It gets cold there. And muggy.

For You

"I did it for you!"
Well, that's not true
You did this
For you
To get a reaction
To gain some traction
To brag or boast
To say you did the most
Your grandiose notions
Were not the right potion
You
Went on a fishing expedition
In the wrong lake
There's no way
On any day of my existence
That I would choose
To entertain such foolishness
You didn't listen
You made up *your* mind
About what I wanted, what I needed
And what I would receive
And now you're mad at *me*?
I can't even begin to dig
Into the insanity presented
I've lost interest in this battle
Of idiotic proportions
That didn't need to happen
I've lost interest
In you

I immensely dislike hearing "I did it for you." Yeah, I dated that guy too. Always doing extreme things. Going to great lengths. Nothing I was remotely interested in. He spent so much time and energy on bullshit, then would get morally fucking offended when I wasn't a sycophant at his feet, foaming with appreciation.

Hey Homie! Don't spend twelve years making me a mohair sweater. I'm allergic. I rarely wear sweaters. How hard is it to ask? I'm using sweaters, but you know what I'm saying, yes?

And PLEASE don't do life changing shit for me. Do it for yourself. Be secure in knowing it's the right thing for you. I don't want your resentment over something I never asked for. You can roll that up tight and jam it somewhere uncomfortable.

Have you met this person? Don't they get on your very last fucking nerve?

Swallowed

Night has come
Swallowed up the sun
The sky a somber tapestry
Stretching the earth
The stars scattered
Like freckles upon its face
Creatures scuttle under cover
Slinking and skulking
Shadows glide with ill intent
Deals made in an unlit alley
Lovers meet in secret
Doing things the daylight shames
The ocean black and motionless
Beckons to the lonely
Come play
The round red moon
Hangs low, glowing
As dark winged things fly
Mortals shudder, disturbed
Their souls reflected back
With no remedy until morn

THIS is also not about THAT.

I'm pretty sure I was a pirate in my prior life. Or maybe just a wench. Who the hell knows?

I love the night and darkness. And I've been around long enough to know that horrors occur whenever they fucking feel like it.

The sun only saves you from vampires. But sadly, not the soul variety, and not day walkers.

Torch

A dark bar
A darker corner
Her voice burns
As it floats across
The lapels of my jacket smoke
My tie chokes
I'm barely breathing
Her dress doesn't cling
It's strangling me
While caressing her
Like a lover
Returned home
After being too long gone
Her lips are a color
That men don't know
But are very curious about
She is killing me
And it isn't soft

I love watching men watch women sing. I can see the fantasy unwind in their minds. The glazed, lustful looks. The total devastation. Desire for a stranger, based on a voice. We all do it. That's how some of the scariest looking, crazy, mean ass mo-fos on this earth have stunning, sane, kind partners. Not to say there isn't something else about them that's great, but we bein real here. And yes, different people are attracted to different things. If you lined up my exes, you might be confused. Looks aren't everything. I mean, you can't look like some eldritch sewer creature and scare small children and be with me, but my idea of attractive starts with the brain.

Anyway! (Not anyways, not ever—and yeah, I ramble.) There are female singers out there whose voices make me think about switching teams. Ooh-whee! If I could rap, I'd put all y'all in a song. Maybe I should write a poem? And hey Lizzo—I love that you're in the universe. Keep on not giving a FUCK what anyone thinks, gurl!

Smile

I heard your smile
From a million miles away
The corners of your lips
Lifted up
I felt the sun
Burn its sweet punishment
Upon my face
Oh, my love!
I smiled along with you
Did you hear me
Smiling too?

Smiles can be as powerful as kisses. No, they can't, but close. A guy I worked with told me my smile was warmer than the sun and a blessing to others. I was stunned and suddenly shy. I didn't know what to say. How do you even respond to a compliment like that?

Thank you seemed insufficient, but I went with it.

The other thing? The more important thing? Have you ever loved someone so much you felt like you could feel them, even if they weren't there?

Ice Queen

The snow is ripping
Through the holes
In my soul
I am gasping, aching
Regrettably wet
Shivering
In an arctic cold
Unprepared
For this frozen landscape
Stumbling and mumbling
Unable to speak
Not caring
How weak I become
Only wanting
To remove my clothes
And sleep
Find a peaceful dream
To lean upon
Until the Ice Queen comes
To bear me away
On her crystalline sleigh
But she is a hateful mistress
Who may deny me reprieve
From the unrelenting freeze
When I wake
Believing it to be
A fevered dream
I sigh in relief
Only to see puddles
Forming at my feet

One time, I woke up around dark o'clock a.m. freezing to death. I was so cold it hurt. I was shuddering and scared out of my mind. I thought I had been taken somehow and put in a freezer.

Then I woke up again. Warm. Socks on. Uncurled.

Has this ever happened to anyoneay'all or am I the only fucking weirdo?

That's not when I wrote this though, just brings it to mind.

I wrote this after my heart was blasted into fragments. I felt more alone and isolated than I ever had before. It was the closest I'd ever been to depression. I wanted to give up. One day I will share why, but I can't bring myself to just yet. I'm sure that's disappointing to read, but this ain't a tell all y'all. Vol II! You hate me, don't you?

PS: Have you ever noticed that the shattered pieces weigh so much more than your whole heart?

What's Up

Book in my hand
Your head in my lap
I'm reading you some story
Dragons, knights, fairies, and kings
On an old park bench
Emotions roll over me
A blend of happy things
This level of joy
Until now, has been unknown
And what we're doing
Doesn't seem like much
A book and a bench
Some flowers and trees
So what?
But you are here
With me, my dearest
And that's what's up

The simplest things make me extremely happy. A book. Time with a friend. The ocean. Mountains. Catching stars in my telescope. Flowers. Storms. Fresh laundry.

Caught in a warm rain. A song. I wrote this after looking at Venus one night.

In need of recharge
I laid my chest
Open to the moon
And silver stars
As Venus looked on
I let my heart rest!
And when I again
Had the organ
Beneath my breast
Filled with stardust
And moon beams
I rose
Renewed

Another thing that makes me happy? Solitude.

I'm contrary that way. I love my people, but I also love to be alone. Originally my solitude was forced, but now I crave it. I truly enjoy time to myself. No TV, no phone, no computer, no other people. Sometimes I'm a jerk when I don't get it. Kinda like food.

People don't understand this about me, and I don't know how to help with that. I'm okay alone and I'm okay being social. I'm not mad if you haven't sent me a text or called. I'm not wondering if you're still my friend, if you still care. There are exceptions, but for the most part? I'm cool.

Game Over

While it was fun for a minute
I'm no longer interested
In the games you play
The Oregon trail has gone stale
No new scents to sense
No adventure around the corner
No great tales to tell
Pack it in, take a hike
Go somewhere and fly a kite
The ghosts caught up to you
Asteroids smashed your ship
A barrel rolled you over
Castle Fynn was taken again
That maiden was a demon
Liu Kang's victory was flawless
Your Kalimdor quest
Was not your best
Your avatar went off a cliff
Geralt thinks you're a bitch
No cheat in the manual
No extra men
No phoning friends
A Fortnite has come and gone
The bonus rounds are none
Thank you *ever so* for playing
Revan will see you out
As your turn is done

Briefly dated a gamer. Won't evah do that again. At least not without knowing exactly how deep in he is. When you tell a woman you gotta finish your game before you guys can eat or, umm, do other things, I canNOT be that woman. Especially not if it's more than 45 minutes. I need food. And those other things. Stat. I will cut you. I'd rather you just ask me to play Mortal Kombat. We don't need to date.

Goat

When I saw a little black goat
Looking at me through my window
I assumed I was not quite awake
It was very early in the day
I rubbed my eyes, but nothing changed
My bemused confusion grew when
Another goat, white this time, joined
My little black friend and believe it or not
They were met by a little black chicken
Lot of little and lots of critters for such an hour
Which made me feel a lil bit disturbed
Because I live in the suburbs and while
There are many dogs and cats, and even birds
Goats and chickens don't quite fit
I called Ginger to ask her what the truck
And surely enough, our lovely new neighbor
Had bought them as pets
I realized I needed a little more sleep
Before I dealt with the menagerie

True story. Sleep brain could not figure out why in the entire universe there were baby goats and chickens in my backyard. My rottie was confused too. She just said there tilting her pretty doggie head. I saw them four or five more times in my yard. They were cute.

Goats do this hoppy thing that cracks me up. We all accepted that baby goats and chickens were a thing now. The little white goat semi head-butted my rottie. She was 98lbs at the time. I think the goat was maybe 30 lbs. No harm.

One day I find out the asshole at the end of the street had killed one of the little baby goats. Why? He was tired of them getting into his yard. Seriously, dude? A baby goat? Oh no! Not that! What a sniveling twat. Lousy, useless motherfucker!

It made me sad and angry. The poor owner was beyond upset. The whole neighborhood wanted to beat his ass. It got bad. He was fined and arrested. Piece of shit. He ended up moving away. I'm still mad at that jackass.

UberXL

December 20, 2021
Goshen, Ohio
Why am I even out here? Stupid hillbillies. Stupid cornfield. A bonfire they said. So much fun. I should kick all their fucking throats. Waste of my fucking time. Drunk morons stomping around, being, well, drunk. Joy. Can I even *get* an Uber out in these stupid fucking sticks? UGH. I hit the icon on my iPhone.

After a million godforsaken years, a silver SUV pulls up. I did not order an SUV and I'm not paying for it.

"Shannon?" The driver, a tall, slender white man, asks from behind the wheel.

"Yeah, but I didn't order an X. I'm not paying for an upgrade," I tell him, shivering. I'm getting in this thing no matter what, though. I'm frozen and irritated. Bad combination.

"No problem. Your first driver got a flat. I came instead."

I pause and look at him. Nope, not Nilesh but whatever. Uber is Uber.

I get in the back and Mike, according to his dashboard nametag, asks all these questions I grunt no to. I do not want to chat.

"You're really pretty," he says, this eyeing me in the rearview.

I thank him, putting as much fuck off and boredom in my voice as possible.

"No, I mean really, really pretty. You ever model?"

"Seriously? That line stopped working before we were born."

"I bet you wouldn't go out with an Uber driver, would you?"

"Wellll, I don't have anything *against* Uber drivers."

"I bet you're stuck up."

"Whatever dude, just drive."

"You know what else I think?"

"Don't know, don't give a fuck, zero-star ride. Can you just *not*?"

We ride in beautiful silence for all of three minutes before Mike starts up again. This fucking guy.

"I think we're going to have so much fun together, Shannon. Special fun. Special time. You're perfect for me. Perfect. See that camera up there?" he says pointing. "Once we're done, the world will know how much prettier your insides are compared to your outside."

December 23, 2021
Tucson, Arizona
The Uber pulls up. It's a black SUV. I did not order that and I'm not paying.

"Gina?" The driver, a tall, nice-looking woman asks from behind the wheel.

"Yeah, but I didn't order an SUV, I don't want to be char—"

"No problem. Your other driver got a flat. I came instead."

I pause and look at her. Her dashboard tag says Shannon. Shannon it is.

I climb in the back. The radio is talking about two Uber drivers they found. One decayed, one horribly mutilated in some small Ohio town. It's been national news all day.

"Can you believe that?" I ask Shannon. "People are crazy. You should be careful."

"Oh, I'm always careful. Don't worry your pretty head about me."

Shannon has a nice smile. We ride in beautiful silence for about three minutes.

"Hey Gina, you ever been to Mexico?" This fucking bitch.

I love the idea of a killer being killed by a bigger psycho, or someone who just snaps because they have had enough. So delightful!

The really uglyangrysad, one word, part of me used to wish the whole lot of my abusers and tormentors would get Chainsaw Massacred or some shit. Now, I've got not one single solitary fuck to give about any of them.

Captive Audience

Dear Ms. Nash,

If you are reading this, you are undoubtedly awake. Please do not be alarmed. You are not a hostage, but merely our guest. You will find your suite of rooms well appointed, comfortable, and relaxing. You have access to books, music, movies, television, and any items you may require. Any medications have been brought from your residence. You will find them in your bathroom.

Your stay here is required and for your own safety. On the table in your sitting room is a computer. Please use the computer to type up a list of items you need and would like to have during your stay with us.

Shopping will be done every Monday and your items will arrive early the next evening.

The computer has limited resources. You will only be allowed to communicate with other guests and the management in the facility. We encourage you to make friends with your fellow guests. It will make your stay that much more pleasant.

Your activity is monitored 24/7. Do not attempt to leave. Do not attempt to contact anyone outside the facility. There are swift and strict security measures in place to discourage any such activity.

We want your stay to be uneventful and we sincerely wish to avoid any incidents.

Thank you,
The Management

Do you originally think it's a joke and play along?

- *Do you try to escape?*
- *Do you form friendships? Trust anyone?*
- *How long until you get complacent?*
- *What items would you request?*
- *Would you refuse items?*
- *Would you ask for ridiculous things to see if "they" comply?*
- *How would you have this end?*

You don't have to play at all, but I hope you will. Email me!

The End

You made it through? Congratulations! I truly thank you for reading. I hope you got something out of it. Anything. Even just a little chuckle. A shake of the head. If you didn't, that's okay too. Just don't be a keyboard cowperson about it. Be cool, baby. Be cool. Yup, Tarantino fan!

The song list:

Blown Away: Akon
Fool in the Rain: Led Zeppelin
Go Down Once More: Phantom of the Opera/Andrew Lloyd Webber
Sunshine: Lupe Fiasco
Valerie: Amy Winehouse (cover)
Come on By: Vintage Trouble
Mother: Danzig
Layla: Eric Clapton
Sexy MF: Prince
Kiss: Prince
Garden: Pearl Jam
1812 Overture: Tchaikovsky
Photographs and Memories: Jim Croce
Ribbons in the Sky: Stevie Wonder
All Along the Watchtower: Jimi Hendrix (cover)
Predator: Ice Cube
Wild is the Wind: Nina Simone
Baby It's Cold Outside: Ray Charles (cover)
Banana Pancakes: Jack Johnson
Little Man You've Had A Busy Day: Sarah Vaughan (cover)
Power of Equality: Red Hot Chili Peppers
Some other songs came in, but I couldn't make them fit without making the poem more ridiculous than it already was.

Next time …!

When not to be a dick!
Jazz, Blues, and Tupac
My mama n'em
Bitch Switch
More poems and stories and a deeper dive into my experiences

Extras!

DO NOT READ THESE LAST TWO IF A TEENY TINY LITTLE BIT OF 'SMUT' BOTHERS YOU.

Love Thy Neighbor

Wednesday, August 2

Michael: There she is again, at the window. Her tits pushing out from one of the many skimpy nightdresses she wears. She stands there just fucking breathing. My stupid cock throbs with every breath she takes. When she turns from the window, I can see the barest hint of her round ass. Bitch. How would she feel if I waltzed in and bent her over that ugly fucking chair her husband brought home. Would she fight me? Cry? Call me names while I pounded into her? I laugh then. I sound like some kind of psycho. I would never. Why does she make me think these thoughts? I don't want to hurt her. I just want her and it's bad. It annoys me when Chelsea calls me to come to bed.

Sophia: There he is again, at the window. He's watching me, I know. He must like the nightdresses. I like when he watches. I want to show him more, but I don't dare. I can feel myself throbbing with every breath I take. I have to turn away. Asshole. Why doesn't he just waltz in and bend me over this ugly fucking chair Jonah brought home? I could pretend to fight him. Cry! Call him names while he pounds into me. I laugh then. I must be crazy! Why does he make me think these thoughts? And what about his wife? Chelsea.

I hate her, I think. I just want him and it's bad. It annoys me when Jonah calls me to come to bed.

Thursday, August 3

Michael: I watch her husband leave with a suitcase. Jonah. Such a tall, serious looking man. I've never seen him smile. Not even when Chelsea took him her famous chocolate chip pecan pie. How did he end up with Sophia? He's so stuffy. Chelsea won't be back for a couple days, I wonder…

Sophia: Jonah of the buttons is leaving. Can he breathe in that thing? When did he become so stiff everywhere except where I need him to be? Where is Chelsea? I wonder…

Jonah: I cannot wait to get away from Sophia. She thinks I don't know. How stupid she is. Showing her tits to that idiot Michael. I can't wait to see Chelsea.

Dry

Your lies
Made my kitty dry
A million licks
Couldn't fix it
From juicy grape
To desiccated raisin
From warm rain
To barren drought
Well, that's not how she
Wants to be treated
She asked if I
Would find someone else
To pet her
I'm glad to comply
Boy, bye